INVESTIGATIVE AND FORENSIC INTERVIEWING

A Personality-focused Approach

INVESTIGATIVE AND FORENSIC INTERVIEWING

A Personality-focused Approach

Craig N. Ackley
Shannon M. Mack
Kristen Beyer
Philip Erdberg

CRC Press
Taylor & Francis Group
Boca Raton   London   New York

CRC Press is an imprint of the
Taylor & Francis Group, an **informa** business

CRC Press
Taylor & Francis Group
6000 Broken Sound Parkway NW, Suite 300
Boca Raton, FL 33487-2742

International Standard Book Number: 978-1-4200-8425-2 (Hardback)

Library of Congress Cataloging-in-Publication Data

Forensic interviewing and personality disorders / Philip Erdberg ... [et al.].
    p. cm.
  Includes bibliographical references and index.
  ISBN 978-1-4200-8425-2 (hbk. : alk. paper)
    1. Interviewing in law enforcement--Psychological aspects. 2. Personality
assessment. 3. Personality disorders. 4. Forensic psychology. I. Erdberg, Philip. II.
Title.

HV8073.3.F67 2011
614'.15--dc22   2010033012

Visit the Taylor & Francis Web site at
http://www.taylorandfrancis.com

and the CRC Press Web site at
http://www.crcpress.com

Contents

About the Authors

Craig N. Ackley, M.S., is a former supervisory special agent with the FBI. He retired from the Behavioral Analysis Unit (BAU) of the FBI's National Center for the Analysis of Violent Crime where he provided psychological and behavioral support primarily in the areas of sexual assault, domestic violence, stalking, and homicide. He is currently the president of Behavioral Science Education and Consultation Services, Inc.

Shannon McAuliffe Mack, M.A., is a former senior research analyst with the FBI's National Center for the Analysis of Violent Crime where she provided research support and case-specific operational assistance. She is currently vice president of Behavioral Science Education and Consultation Services, Inc., where she provides operational assistance and training in the areas of trial strategy, interview strategy, and case analysis.

Kristen Beyer, Ph.D., is a licensed clinical psychologist who formerly worked in the FBI's National Center for the Analysis of Violent Crime as the supervisory social/behavioral science research coordinator where she provided consultation, training, and research on violent crime matters. She is currently a consultant with Behavioral Science Education and Consultation Services, Inc. and an adjunct professor.

Philip Erdberg, PhD, is a diplomate in clinical psychology of the American Board of Professional Psychology. He is a past president of the Society for Personality Assessment, the 1995 recipient of the Society's Distinguished Contribution Award, and the 2001 recipient of the Outstanding Achievement Award of the Forensic Mental Health Association of California. He consults in a variety of school, clinical, correctional, and law enforcement settings and is a frequent workshop presenter.

1

INTRODUCTION

Purpose of This Book

The purpose of this book is to show how taking an interviewee's personality into account can lead to a more productive interview outcome. Our goal is to provide a window into the personality types most commonly encountered in the legal system and to demonstrate how to use this insight to plan and conduct effective interviews. Our experience suggests that this personality-focused approach is helpful for forensic professionals in a variety of areas: law enforcement officers, attorneys, probation and parole officers, mental health workers, and others who interview witnesses, suspects, and offenders throughout the legal system. Students in criminal justice and forensic psychology programs will also benefit from integrating this approach as they prepare for their careers.

When we think about people, we usually describe them in terms of combinations of traits. One person is described as outgoing and adventurous, another as reserved and deliberate. That is what personality is: the combination of traits that makes each of us unique. At their extremes, some of these traits can cause people difficulty. Too much adventurousness can lead to risky and dangerous behavior; too much deliberateness can immobilize a person.

The *Diagnostic and Statistical Manual of Mental Disorders* ([DSM-IV-TR]; American Psychiatric Association, 2000) presents a categorical system of 10 personality disorders that represent the maladaptive extremes when traits like perfectionism or self-centeredness interfere with the person's ability to function effectively at work or in social or interpersonal settings. As an example, one of the criteria for Antisocial

Personality Disorder is that the individual frequently violates social norms with behavior that could lead to arrest.

The information in this book is not intended to be used for diagnosing personality disorders. Instead, we discuss personality in terms of a combination of core traits, with the recognition that any particular personality, as well as the individual traits that comprise it, can fall anywhere on a continuum from mild to extreme. We describe the distinguishing features of each personality as well as any similarities to other personalities. The following are personalities commonly encountered in forensic settings:

- Narcissistic
- Antisocial
- Psychopathic
- Borderline
- Inadequate/Immature
- Paranoid
- Schizotypal

While this book is designed for use by a variety of forensic professionals, its format is specifically crafted for the law enforcement interview. Our experience suggests that an accurate assessment of an interviewee's personality can help in planning and conducting such interviews.

How to Use This Book

Each chapter has the same organizational structure. We begin by providing a basic description of the personality, ways in which to assess if the individual you will be interviewing possesses that particular personality, issues that are important as you prepare for the interview, and suggestions about conducting the interview itself. This organizational structure is described in detail below.

Vignette

Each chapter begins with a vignette of an interviewee you might encounter in a forensic setting. The purpose of the vignette is to illustrate some of the primary features of the personality described within the chapter.

Description of the Personality

This section provides a description of the personality in practical language. We discuss how these individuals view themselves, others, and the world around them, and how these views lead to the behaviors in which they engage. We conclude this section with a summary of the primary features of the personality. As you read this section, begin to think about the implications of that particular personality for the interview setting and for the development of potential interview themes and strategies.

Assessing the Individual

This section is intended for those situations in which you have the opportunity to conduct an indirect assessment of the interviewee prior to the interview. An indirect assessment involves obtaining information about the interviewee in ways other than directly from the interviewee. As noted above, you can conceptualize a maladaptive personality as those characteristics of an individual that continually cause problems in his or her relationships with others, whether in work, social, or interpersonal settings. Therefore, the most valuable sources of information regarding personality will typically be interviews with individuals who know the interviewee, such as current or former intimate partners, family members, friends, associates, and coworkers.

This section provides specific questions pertaining to the personality described in the chapter that can be answered through interviews, as well as through additional sources of information, such as

- Educational records
- Financial records
- DMV records
- Employment records
- Mental health records
- Adult and juvenile criminal records

- Investigative case files (if the interviewee has been previously interviewed)
- Civil court records

Preparation Issues

This section is intended to provide you with a survey of issues that are important to consider as you prepare for the interview.

Understanding Your Reactions to the Individual   This subsection describes the behaviors you are likely to encounter within the interview setting, the motivations behind those behaviors, and instinctive ways in which you are likely to respond. Understanding the behaviors you are likely to encounter and the responses those behaviors are likely to provoke is very important as you prepare for the interview.

Who Should Conduct the Interview   Understanding the personality of the interviewee and what you are likely to encounter within the interview setting is critical to conducting an effective interview. However, it is equally critical that you possess the right combination of personality traits or features necessary to increase the likelihood of things going well. This subsection discusses the features and qualities to consider when determining who the most appropriate interviewer would be.

Number of Interviewers   As the heading suggests, this subsection discusses the number of interviewers recommended for the given personality as well as the reasons behind those suggestions. For law enforcement officers, the number of interviewers may be dictated by agency or jurisdictional policy. In such cases, policy would obviously take precedence.

Physical Space/Environment/Interpersonal Space   This subsection details considerations (when relevant) relating to location of the interview, the setup of the interview room, and what kind of interpersonal space will be most comfortable for the interviewee. For law enforcement officers, the location of the interview will depend on a number of variables such as arrest status, custodial status, agency or jurisdictional policies, time, and resources. In addition, options regarding the setup of the interview room may also be limited. These are suggestions to take into account when you have the ability to do so.

Nonverbal Behavior This subsection discusses the need to be aware of nonverbal behavior—including such things as gestures, eye contact, facial expressions, and posture—that may be relevant to a particular personality. For some personalities, the interviewer's nonverbal behavior may have little impact, while for others it can play a crucial role.

Questions This subsection discusses the nature of the interview questions in terms of such things as scripted versus nonscripted, open-ended versus closed, simple versus compound, and the manner in which they are asked. Again, for some personalities, the nature of the questions may have little relevance, whereas for others it could have serious implications.

Recording the Interview (Notetaking, Audio/Video Recording) This subsection addresses pertinent issues related to notetaking and audio/video recording. It provides guidance on notetaking, in terms of when it is appropriate, whose responsibility it should be and why, how to approach the issue with the interviewee, and how to use notetaking as a tool in the interview process. Regarding audio/visual recording, it provides guidance on when it is necessary and why, as well as how to approach the issue with the interviewee. The suggestions provided in this subsection are intended for those cases where audio or video recording is left to the discretion of the interviewer. For law enforcement officers, the use of audio/video recording may be determined by agency and jurisdictional policy. Prior to any interview, agency policies and jurisdictional laws should be reviewed to ensure adherence.

The Interview

In this section we take many of the key issues emphasized throughout the chapter and apply them to the actual interview through discussion and examples based on the opening vignette. It is not meant to be a comprehensive discussion of all that you may encounter during the actual interview. However, it does integrate many of the issues that are important for increasing the likelihood of the interview going well for that particular personality.

Key Points to Remember

We conclude each chapter by summarizing key things you should and should not do as a function of the interviewee's personality.

Interview versus Interrogation

As previously stated, this book focuses on the law enforcement interview (*not* the interrogation) and how understanding the personality of the interviewee is critical to the interview process. As such, we need to make an important distinction between *interview* and *interrogation*.

An *interview* is nonaccusatory in nature and primarily involves gathering information. This is the time for reducing anxiety, developing rapport (when possible), and doing those things that will create a nonthreatening environment in which the interviewee feels willing to talk. It is about gathering information that will assist you in gauging the interviewee's "baseline" behavior, so that you can quickly identify increases in anxiety, anger, or emotionality as the interview progresses. The interview is also about gathering information that can be useful in the interrogation phase and any subsequent legal proceedings.

An *interrogation*, on the other hand, is accusatory and more confrontational in nature. It is a persuasive process in which you are trying to obtain some form of admission or confession from the interviewee. However, once a confession is obtained, the interrogation can take on the feel of an interview in terms of obtaining details. Studies show that most offenders who confess do so right away. However, for the vast majority who do not, the interview provides a better platform for gathering information that can be useful for the investigative and prosecutive processes. The lies, omissions, and inconsistencies you obtain during the interview phase can be useful during the interrogation and, absent a confession, can be invaluable during any subsequent criminal proceedings.

Legal and Policy Considerations

We realize that advisement of rights is always a consideration when questioning a potential suspect in an investigation. At what point an interviewer is required to advise the interviewee of his or her rights depends on a number of factors. Prior to conducting any interview, you should review and understand both agency policies and legal requirements within your jurisdiction regarding advisement of rights.

In addition, ensure that you are familiar with, understand, and are in accordance with the policy and legal requirements within your jurisdiction prior to incorporating any of our suggestions (e.g., audio/visual recording, location of the interview, number of interviewers) or implementing any strategies based on the information in this book.

Reference

American Psychiatric Association. (2000). *Diagnostic and statistical manual of mental disorders* (4th ed., text rev.). Washington, DC: American Psychiatric Association.

2

THE NARCISSISTIC PERSONALITY

Introduction

Aaron Beck (2004) noted that "high self esteem means thinking well of oneself whereas narcissism involves passionately wanting to think well of oneself" (p. 245). At its core, narcissistic personality disorder can be understood as a set of traits motivated by a desire to establish and defend an image as special, unique, or different in some way. But because this self-image usually originates as a defense against intense feelings of vulnerability, it can be fragile and susceptible to insult.

While the popular conception of the narcissistic individual is someone who is arrogant, exhibitionistic, and limelight seeking, that is only one manifestation of this complicated style. Gabbard (1989) described a spectrum of narcissistic types that vary in terms of how the individual relates to others. At one extreme is what Gabbard called the oblivious narcissist, a person whose interpersonal style is characterized by a self-centered and grandiose insensitivity. Because these individuals are oblivious to others, they are largely impervious to insult or criticism. It is the oblivious narcissist whose features most closely parallel the DSM-IV-TR description of narcissistic personality disorder.

At the other extreme of Gabbard's (1989) narcissistic continuum is the person he calls the hypervigilant narcissist. These individuals view themselves as different and entitled to special treatment, not because they are superior and grandiose, but because they are thin-skinned, sensitive, and vulnerable, leaving them endlessly alert to any criticism or insult that questions their "specialness." This is a more covert version of narcissism, and these individuals often present themselves as timid and self-demeaning, even as they expect special consideration from others and become furious when it is not forthcoming.

In this chapter we discuss the prototypical features and behaviors of individuals at the two extremes of the narcissistic continuum. These extreme types are referred to by a number of names. On one end of the continuum is the grandiose, oblivious, overt, or thick-skinned narcissist. At the other end is the hypervigilant, vulnerable, thin-skinned, or covert narcissist. Throughout the remainder of this chapter, and elsewhere in this book, we refer to these two types of narcissistic personalities as the *oblivious* narcissist and the *vulnerable* narcissist.

Keep in mind that many narcissistic individuals exhibit a blend of oblivious and vulnerable traits. However, by understanding the features and behaviors associated with these extreme types, we think you will be better equipped to interview any narcissistic individual, regardless of where he or she falls on the continuum.

The Oblivious Narcissist

Mark Thompson, impeccably dressed as always, entered his office, where all of his accolades were hanging on the wall. Anyone looking at his office would likely describe it as a shrine. It reflected him pretty well: anything to boost his sense of being superior to those around him. After checking his e-mails, he walked to the break room and poured himself a cup of coffee before heading to his morning meeting.

During the meeting, there was some roundtable discussion about accomplishments of various groups and committees. Mark took full advantage of the opportunity to speak, enumerating his accomplishments, going on at length. While he was talking, a couple of coworkers were rolling their eyes as one kept track of the number of times he said "I" or "me" when taking credit for the work of the entire group. Before taking his seat, he asked in a very demanding way, "When are those bonuses going to come through for the last quarter because I heard that Susan got hers and she didn't do half of what I did." Then, in his condescending manner, he went on to say, "I don't even know why she's getting a bonus, but she sure as hell shouldn't be getting one before me." As he sat down, he was completely oblivious to the reactions of his coworkers. He then remembered something else he had wanted to mention and added, "Twice this week someone has been in my parking spot. I don't know who it is that's been parking in my spot and I don't have the time to look into it, but have the secretary send a memo so that whoever it is that's doing it will knock it off."

After work, Mark met Jennifer Davis at a small restaurant, where there was minimal chance of running into anyone they knew. Jennifer worked in the accounting section of the same company where Mark was employed. They had first met at a social function organized by the company and had been having an affair for approximately seven months. Mark was married and insisted on keeping the relationship a secret. They would meet regularly at Jennifer's apartment or at the restaurant. Mark was curious because this time Jennifer had sent him a text, asking him to meet even though it was unplanned. When he got there, she unloaded on him, telling him she needed more from the relationship and demanding that he leave his wife.

Mark didn't want to tell her that she didn't really mean that much to him. He liked her well enough, but he really just enjoyed the attention and adoration. He realized that she was going to jeopardize his reputation, his marriage, and that he needed to do something.

"I'm pregnant," she said. With a look that was clearly a cross between irritation and disbelief, Mark responded, "What? You told me you were on the pill." "I guess I must have forgotten to take it," she responded.

"How could you be so stupid?" he asked with anger in his voice. Tears welled up in her eyes and she didn't reply. Indifferent to her crying, Mark said matter of factly, "We'll just take care of this then." "What do you mean 'take care of this'?" she said. "I'm not getting an abortion, if that's what you mean. I'm having this child and you are going to help provide for it." Mark was irate. "You're getting an abortion and that's the end of it. I'm not going to let you ruin my life this way and lose everything I've worked for." "I told you I'm not getting an abortion!" she yelled. "You're not having that baby. So go home and get yourself together. We'll talk about it tomorrow." With that, Mark got up and walked out of the restaurant, leaving her behind.

The following day, Mark met Jennifer and she immediately told him that not only was she going to keep the baby but that he needed to tell his wife so that he could be a part of the baby's life, regardless of how it affected his marriage or his career. Mark had thought about this encounter all night and contemplated what actions he would take depending on her decision on whether or not to keep the baby. Because she would not agree to the abortion, he was left with only one choice. His next steps were purely manipulative. Mark's response surprised her. He calmly agreed, telling her she was right and that he would support her decision and just asked her not to say anything to anyone until he had a chance to tell his wife first and then they would figure it out from there. He lovingly put his arms around her and apologized for the way he reacted and told her that everything would be okay. While they embraced, he reassured her and told her he was going to go home and figure out how to tell his wife. He said he would call her afterward. Later in the evening he called and told her that it hadn't gone well and asked if she could meet him at their usual place.

The following evening, Jennifer was reported missing by her mother. Subsequent investigation disclosed that Jennifer had confided in a good friend that she was seeing someone. She did not tell her friend the name of the individual, only that he was successful, older, and married. Two days before her disappearance, Jennifer had called her friend and said she was pregnant. She was distraught because she had fallen in love with the man she was seeing and did not know how he was going to react to the pregnancy. She wanted to keep the baby and planned on meeting with him. She was going to tell him that he needed to make a decision between her and his wife. However, regardless of his decision, she was going to keep the baby. During the course of the investigation, the pregnancy was confirmed through medical records. Based on a review of the victim's telephone records and other investigative activity, Mark was identified as working at the same company as the victim and believed to be the man Jennifer had told her friend about.

Description of the Oblivious Narcissist

The current *Diagnostic and Statistical Manual of Mental Disorders* (DSM-IV-TR) includes nine items in its description of Narcissistic Personality Disorder. However, they all revolve around two themes: (1) a "grandiose sense of self importance" (p. 714) and (2) the overt expression of that grandiosity. This description essentially characterizes the oblivious narcissist who, in many ways, represents the most recognizable and least complex manifestation of this personality style. This version of narcissism involves the creation of a grandiose self-image into which the individual escapes from a far less glamorous reality. For the oblivious narcissist, achieving that ideal image becomes the primary focus in his or her life. It is relentlessly pursued at all costs and with complete obliviousness to how his or her actions impact others, until fantasy and reality become one.

The oblivious narcissist's grandiosity leads to an interpersonal style informed by his or her sense of being unique, special, superior, and entitled. These individuals believe they should not be held to the same standards of conduct and courtesy as everyone else, but rather should be allowed a set of rules reflective of the status to which they are entitled. Others should meet their needs, demands, and expectations unquestioningly, no matter how unreasonable. Their feeling of uniqueness also creates the belief that they cannot be understood by anyone other than those who occupy, in their estimation, the same lofty status.

It is difficult to miss obliviously narcissistic individuals as they continually seek the spotlight. But while they may initially appear friendly and even charming, you will soon recognize that you have entered a world that revolves solely around them. Their language is self-referential, typically filled with the pronouns "I" and "me," while they regale you with their virtues and accomplishments. They show only a passing, superficial interest in anything you have to say unless it validates their grandiose self-image. Meaningful relationships consist solely of those "important" people who can sustain or enhance their self-concept. People within the oblivious narcissist's world are there only to serve his or her needs and are welcome to remain as long as they provide adulation and mirroring. However, when they no longer serve those needs, they are summarily dismissed.

Oblivious narcissists treat others in this manner because they typically do not develop meaningful attachments that bring with them emotions such as empathy, guilt, or remorse. Becoming emotionally close to others would risk exposing themselves to feelings that could contradict their idealized self-concept of power and control. Should you be unfortunate enough to inflict a "narcissistic injury" that threatens their feelings of invulnerability—particularly anything that causes shame or humiliation—be prepared for a swift and angry response that is condescending, dismissive, and devaluing. If the insult is severe enough, it can trigger a "narcissistic rage," accompanied by verbal abuse and physical aggression.

In summary, oblivious narcissists have fused fantasy and reality to the point that they *believe* they are special and superior (in terms of wealth, power, brilliance, beauty, ability, etc.), and therefore:

- They are entitled to special treatment and privileges
- They have every reason to expect things that are commensurate with their "specialness" and superiority
- They should not be held to the rules and standards that apply to other people
- They deserve recognition, praise, and admiration
- Other people exist to satisfy their needs
- If others do not recognize how special they are, they should be dismissed or punished
- They neither deserve criticism, nor do others have the right to criticize them
- Only people as special and superior as they are can understand them
- Other people are envious of them
- Others are inferior and do not deserve admiration, special recognition, or high achievements
- They maintain a relatively stable sense of self-esteem until something occurs that threatens to separate fantasy from reality and expose their underlying inadequacies and vulnerabilities
- Any particular belief that is not met or is challenged in any way is intolerable.

Assessing the Oblivious Narcissist

This section is not designed to exhaust all sources of information you might utilize to conduct an indirect assessment of a potential interviewee. Rather, it lists a number of questions that address the core features of oblivious narcissism discussed throughout this chapter and offers some suggestions regarding sources of information typically most useful in answering those questions. These questions are not for the purpose of diagnosing the interviewee with narcissistic personality disorder, but rather for determining the presence and strength of obliviously narcissistic features of his or her personality. For convenience, we have referenced a male interviewee in this section, but the suggestions we make are equally applicable to women.

The central feature of the oblivious narcissist is an all-pervasive sense of superiority, often not supported by actual accomplishments. Therefore, when interviewing friends, family, coworkers, and others, try to determine how he portrays himself:

- Does he believe he is better than everyone around him?
- Does he act superior to those around him?
- Does he feel entitled to special treatment?
- Would others refer to him as self-centered, arrogant, or self-absorbed?
- When talking with others, does he tend to direct the topic of conversation to himself?
- Does what he thinks of himself match reality? Does it accurately reflect who he truly is?

The oblivious narcissist tends not to develop deep emotional relationships because that would risk exposing his vulnerabilities. Instead, he tends to see others as objects that exist to serve his needs as opposed to seeing people as having their own identities. When interviewing collateral individuals, try to find out what his attitudes and behaviors are regarding relationships:

- Does he show a lack of sincere interest in others?
- Do his relationships seem superficial and shallow?
- Does he lack the ability to develop close, emotional relationships?

- Does he seem to associate with people who can promote things that he wants?
- Does he try to associate with people he considers important or special?
- Does he manipulate others or use them for his own ends?

To maintain his inflated self-image, the oblivious narcissist often relies on the feedback of others. Therefore, he behaves in ways designed to elicit responses that boost his ego. So, when talking with others, ask the following:

- Does he constantly say and do things that make it appear he is fishing for compliments or recognition? In other words, do his interactions often involve attempts at getting others to say and do things that reinforce his ego?

Although the oblivious narcissist looks for positive feedback, his self-absorbed behavior and lack of real concern for the feelings of others eventually provokes negative responses. However, when others respond negatively or critically, then they may quickly find themselves on the receiving end of angry, condescending, or dismissive behavior. Find out the following from those with whom he interacts:

- Do people around him tend to get irritated, annoyed, and angry in response to his treatment of them?
- Do people feel that he is insensitive to their needs or wishes?
- When someone criticizes him or injures his identity in any way, does he immediately respond by "bad-mouthing" that person or trying to make that person feel inferior or insignificant?

Although the oblivious narcissist does not believe that rules apply to him, he typically adheres to many of them. It is the price he pays to obtain recognition and admiration. Hand in hand with this is the impulse control and self-discipline needed to do what is necessary to achieve some level of success. This is one of the features that differentiates the oblivious narcissist from the antisocial personality. Although antisocial individuals can display many narcissistic qualities, they typically lack robust impulse control and self-discipline.

- Overall, does he function fairly well?
- Is he somewhat successful or competent at what he does?
- Can he function in work and family environments?
- Is his work and relationship history fairly stable?
- Has he been able to succeed in educational settings (particularly college level)?

While the oblivious narcissist can function fairly well and achieve success within the employment environment, his behavior still reflects his sense of superiority. Make sure to ask about the following when speaking with coworkers or others with whom he works:

- Does he seek recognition for his achievements no matter how small?
- Does he tend to be competitive?
- Would he rather take credit for work than share it?
- Would others consider him a team player?
- Is he a sore loser?
- When someone else does something well or receives recognition, does he diminish it or dismiss it in some way?
- Does he put all his accomplishments on display for others to see (e.g., plaques and awards on the wall)?

Preparation Issues

Preparation is a critical aspect of any interview. This section is intended to provide an understanding of those issues that are important as you prepare to interview the oblivious narcissist.

Understanding Your Reactions to the Individual

Before conducting the interview, it is important to understand the instinctive ways in which you are likely to respond to the interviewee. The centerpiece of oblivious narcissism is a sense of superiority in both thought and behavior. These individuals seek validation of their superiority from other people. When you fail to provide that or, worse, when you threaten their identity in some way, they often resort to behavior that is condescending, sarcastic, or dismissive in order to reestablish their superiority. The natural tendency for most people is to become irritated, frustrated, angry, or defensive in the face of such behavior. It is critical that you understand that these dismissive strategies work to maintain self-esteem and a grandiose image. Anticipating the possibility of this type of behavior enhances your ability to maintain your composure and not to respond in negative ways.

There is also a power differential issue that can present a unique challenge in the law enforcement interview setting. The oblivious narcissist must continually be in a "one-up" position, asserting superiority, dominance, and control. However, this also happens to be the exact position that many law enforcement officers instinctively try to establish and maintain within the interview setting. Although you might feel a strong urge to let the interviewee know that you are the one in charge and that you "hold all the cards," it is important to resist that urge. Oblivious narcissists like to feel they have the upper hand. If you are drawn into a fight for control, that conflict will become the focus of an interview that is less likely to be productive.

While we described above how oblivious narcissists typically behave, that may not always be the case. Although they do not believe that rules apply to them, in many instances they adhere to those rules (or give the appearance of doing so) because it is advantageous. Within the interview setting, they may appear cooperative and willing to talk to you. Keep in mind that this "cooperative" attitude is because it is advantageous to them and typically lasts only as long as they are not directly challenged or confronted. So, always be prepared for the dismissive and condescending behavior we have described—even if they initially appear friendly and cooperative.

Who Should Conduct the Interview

Understanding the oblivious narcissist and what you are likely to encounter is critical to conducting an effective interview. It is equally critical that you possess the right combination of personality traits, given the information we have presented in order to have the best chance of a successful outcome.

The oblivious narcissist has a need to feel in control. Therefore, the interviewer should be someone who is comfortable giving up perceived control and who possesses the ability to keep his or her ego in check. As previously discussed, oblivious narcissists are most comfortable when their grandiose self-image and sense of superiority are not being challenged.

The interview of the oblivious narcissist is not the place for a thin-skinned or emotionally volatile individual. Showing negative emotions (e.g., anger, defensiveness, frustration, or boredom) can interfere with your ability to conduct an effective interview. It can also start you along the path of being confrontational and ultimately shutting down the interview. Giving the interviewee any indication that you are experiencing positive emotions (e.g., satisfaction when catching him in a lie or when the interview is going your way) can also be problematic because it gives the appearance of a change in the power differential. Therefore, the interviewer must possess the ability to remain calm, neutral, and to keep his or her emotions in check, resisting the urge to react either verbally or nonverbally.

This kind of interview can be grueling and requires an interviewer with a lot of patience. It can be lengthy because of its methodical and detailed nature, especially because we recommend not challenging or confronting the interviewee. In addition, there is the possibility that you will experience a wider range of emotions with these individuals than with other personalities. This is because not only do you have to deal with what you might experience in response to how they typically behave, but also because of the additional emotions you will experience by continually placing yourself in a subordinate role.

Finally, it is critical that the interviewer be someone who knows the case well and has the ability to recall details with tremendous accuracy within an interview that can be very fluid. It is equally important to retain and recall anything said by the interviewee in order to subtly direct the questioning.

Gender and age can become important factors in the context of a specific interviewee. In general, however, if you possess the qualities described above, these factors are typically not critical.

As you can see, a thoughtful self-evaluation on the part of the interviewer is important. Typically, the law enforcement officer who is assigned the case is likely to conduct the interview. If, however, it is determined that someone else would be better suited, that determination should take precedence in order to increase the likelihood of the interview's success.

Number of Interviewers

It is recommended that you have only one interviewer because of the oblivious narcissist's need to feel in control. The fewer the number of interviewers, the easier it is for the interviewee to see himself as controlling the interaction. If, however, there are two interviewers, one should be designated as primary while the second should be solely responsible for taking notes. We would strongly discourage involving more than two interviewers.

Physical Space/Environment/Interpersonal Space

If you have the luxury of conducting the interview away from a law enforcement facility, you should choose one that does not appear to give you an advantage. Because of the narcissist's sense of superiority and awareness of anything that threatens it, it is recommended that the interview environment not reflect anything that implies a power differential in your favor. For example, you do not want to hold the interview in a setting where the person would be surrounded by symbols of your power and authority (e.g., plaques, flags). Along the same lines, it is best if the interviewer(s) dress in civilian clothes and refrain from having badges, weapons, and insignia visible to the interviewee. Oblivious narcissists avoid intimacy because it is threatening. Therefore, you do not want to invade their personal space during the interview. You can set up the room in a number of ways, to include a table between you and the interviewee, or appropriate space if you are only using chairs.

Nonverbal Behavior

The important thing to remember is that you do not want your nonverbal behavior to suggest what you are feeling about any particular issue. Do not let your behavior indicate any negative emotions (e.g., defensiveness, anger) or any positive emotions (e.g., satisfaction, smugness) that you may experience during the course of the interview. In addition, your nonverbal behaviors should convey the message that you are listening and interested without being overly friendly or intimate. Also, you do not want your nonverbal behaviors to be interpreted as aggressive, confrontational, or challenging.

Questions

Because of the oblivious narcissist's confidence in his or her ability to explain any behavior that is questioned, the goal is to create an environment in which the person is willing to talk. Therefore, questions should be nonconfrontational, contain noninflammatory language, and be open-ended so as to elicit narrative responses.

Recording the Interview (Notetaking, Audio/Video Recording)

Notetaking accomplishes different things in different settings with different types of individuals. With the oblivious narcissist, notetaking allows you to maintain structure, be methodical and detail oriented, and regulate the pace of the interview. Audio and video recording is recommended. It should be addressed as a matter of policy in order to ensure the accuracy of the interview. Regardless of whether you use audio or video recording, notetaking is still recommended as a way of maintaining control of the interview.

Time Frame

Serious consideration should be given to conducting several interviews of the oblivious narcissist, if possible. In any event, you should plan to set aside a good block of time. Anticipate a long, thorough, slow-paced interview that allows you to document as much detail as possible.

The Interview

Now that you have a good understanding of the behaviors that oblivious narcissists are likely to engage in and the reasons for those behaviors, settled on an effective interview style, and engaged in thorough preparation, it's time for the actual interview. This section cannot be a comprehensive summary of everything you may encounter, but it will address many of the details that increase the likelihood of the interview going well. In this section we use the vignette of Mark presented earlier to emphasize key points made throughout this subchapter.

As previously discussed, oblivious narcissists are most comfortable when their grandiose self-image and sense of superiority are not being challenged. One of the ways in which they maintain that comfort is through control of the environment. At least during the initial stages of the interview, you do not want to challenge that control, allowing the interviewee's sense of comfort and superiority to remain intact. Oblivious narcissists often feel they have the ability to explain away any behavior, particularly if they see themselves as occupying a position of superiority. So, allowing interviewees to hold that position will create an environment in which they feel confident in their ability to describe and explain their behavior.

Supporting the interviewee's sense of control begins with the manner in which you arrange the interview. Consider the following example in the case of Mark:

Interviewer (telephonic): Mr. Thompson?
Mr. Thompson: Yes?
Interviewer: Good morning, Mr. Thompson. My name is Dan Martin and I am with the Police Department. I am sorry to bother you, but I am working on a case of a young woman who has been reported missing. Her name is Jennifer Davis. I am trying to talk to anyone who might know her, and your name and number are in her address book. I know you probably have a lot going on, but could you possibly meet with me sometime this afternoon or after work; whichever is more convenient for you?

Language similar to that in the above example begins the interviewer/interviewee relationship in a nonthreatening way, appeals to his sense of importance and superiority, and provides him with a feeling of control while also placing some parameters on that control. You need to identify who you are and what your purpose is in contacting him. A friendly greeting in which you identify yourself not by title, but by your relationship to your agency, allows you to introduce yourself in way that places more emphasis on the relationship with your agency than on yourself. Leaving out your title (e.g., officer, detective, investigator, sergeant, lieutenant) and unit of assignment (e.g., homicide unit) is both less threatening and a subtle way of decreasing your self-importance. The purpose of the contact is also stated in a nonthreatening way. Language such as "I am working on a case...," "Her name *is*...," and "I am trying to talk to anyone who might *know* her" conveys a far less threatening and ominous impression than language such as "I am investigating the disappearance of...," "Her name *was*...," and "I am trying to talk to anyone who might *have known* her." Phrases such as "I am sorry to bother you" and "I know you probably have a lot going on" serve the purpose of appealing to his self-importance. Finally, giving him the choice of when to meet gives him a feeling of control. However, by limiting his options, you are setting the parameters of that control.

At the time of the interview, you want to greet the interviewee in a friendly but deferential way:

Interviewer: Good morning, Mr. Thompson. Or would you prefer to be called something else? *(pause)* I hope this isn't too much of an inconvenience for you?

As discussed elsewhere in this book, addressing the interviewee by his last name *and* asking how he would like to be addressed sets a tone of respect, maintains emotional distance, and provides the interviewee with an initial sense of some control, all of which are important to the oblivious narcissist. In addition, the combination of the above question creates the first opportunity in the interview process to elicit responses that may provide some insight into the underlying personality structure of the interviewee. For the oblivious narcissist, this is your first chance to gauge his tone, demeanor, attitude, and level of willingness to be cooperative. If you get something like, "Oh, it's no problem at all. I just hope I can help" versus, "Actually, it *is* an inconvenience. I don't have anything to tell you so I don't know why you're taking up my time," you have an immediate indication of how the interview is likely to go.

As the interview begins, take your time gathering biographical and background information. Not only does this slow-paced approach allow you to settle into an interview style that is nonthreatening and nonconfrontational, but it also gives you the opportunity to provide identity-enhancing feedback. You can do this in several ways. One is by accommodating his needs and requests (e.g., getting him coffee, asking if he would like to take a break), and the other is through periodically responding in ways that recognize what he believes about himself without being overtly flattering. For example,

Interviewer: What is your home address?
Mr. Thompson: 16324 Crestview Lane.
Interviewer: That's in the River Oaks Subdivision, isn't it?
Mr. Thompson: Yes.
Interviewer: Those are beautiful homes; a little out of my range.

Very simple statements like the one above reinforce the interviewee's sense of superiority. Oblivious narcissists miss nothing that validates what they believe about themselves. So by taking the opportunity to incorporate an indirect compliment, you are providing that validation. The example above may seem like an incidental comment. However, it is that kind of simple statement that accomplishes your goal of allowing the person to stay in his comfort zone. Taking your time during this phase also gives you the chance to gather potentially valuable information concerning relationships and other areas of his life that may provide you some insight as to what is important to him. This information can become useful in the development of any potential interrogation themes or strategies.

Keep in mind that there is a difference between not asserting control of the interview and giving up control of the interview. We are not suggesting that you give up control, only that you allow the interviewee's sense of being in control to go unchallenged. You still maintain control through the direction and manner of the questions and through notetaking, which allows you to maintain structure, be detailed, and regulate the pace. Notetaking is a particularly useful tool with the oblivious narcissist. This goes hand in hand with an in-depth knowledge of the facts of your case and your ability to accurately assess and recall information provided by the interviewee. You can do this through a combination of closed-ended questions that request specific information and open-ended questions that ask for more of a narrative. In addition, you can maintain control by periodically returning to issues that have been previously discussed. The following sequence employs a variety of question types:

Interviewer: How do you know Ms. Davis?

Mr. Thompson: I know her from work. I manage major development projects and she works in the accounting department. I have to deal with her quite often on funding issues.

Interviewer: Are you friends as well? I mean does she feel close enough to confide in you about anything that might be troubling her, or any problems she might be having?

The two questions posed by the interviewer are both closed-ended and information-seeking, using language that is present tense and nonthreatening. Questions such as these give no indication of the information you have in your possession or the direction in which you ultimately want to take the interview. In addition, while both are closed-ended, the second question is clearly much more complex than the first and has a different impact on the interviewee. Oblivious narcissists tend to continually assess information in terms of what is most advantageous to them. Within the interview setting, this means thinking about the specific question posed at the moment and anticipating the direction of the interview and possible lines of questioning. From the interviewee's response to the first question, you might instinctively want to ask another simple, closed-ended, follow-up question such as, "Did you have a relationship with her outside of work?" or "Was your relationship more than just coworkers?" However, by structuring it in a more complex way, you create a different effect. The second question is now focused on the victim, rather than on the interviewee, and the word "relationship" is left out. This is certainly less threatening. However, you have also introduced the issue of the victim possibly confiding in somebody else. Altogether, you have subtly exerted control, limiting his ability to accurately anticipate the direction of the interview and causing him to evaluate more information regarding how he chooses to define his relationship with the victim in response to the second question. Continuing on:

Mr. Thompson: I wouldn't say we are good friends. We speak often about financial issues surrounding the projects I manage, but we don't talk that much about personal issues.

Interviewer: The last time you spoke to her, did she mention anything that, looking back, would cause you concern; or did she sound upset or different in any way?

Mr. Thompson: No, nothing comes to mind. I don't remember her saying anything that caused me concern in any way.

Interviewer: You said you work with her on projects you manage. What kind of projects are they?

Mr. Thompson: We develop analytic software and I make sure each program is developed according to the specifications of the client.

Interviewer: What is analytic software?

Mr. Thompson: It's pretty complicated. In essence, it is software that is used in analyzing different types of data.

Interviewer: Sounds complex. What is Ms. Davis' job with these projects?

Mr. Thompson: She makes sure…

Interview continues for approximately ten minutes, then:

Interviewer: I'm sorry Mr. Thompson; I need to back up here a second just to get caught up in my notes. Sometimes I wish I had someone to take notes for me (smile). When we talked about the last time you spoke with Ms. Davis, I meant to ask, when was that?

Mr. Thompson: Let me think a second. I believe it was last Tuesday (two days before the victim was reported missing).

Interviewer: Did you speak to her in person, or was that over the phone?

Mr. Thompson: I think it was over the phone.

Interviewer: I know you said you didn't recall her saying anything that caused you any concern, but maybe there was something there that could help me in some way. What did she talk about?

As previously stated, within the interview setting, oblivious narcissists attend to the information of the moment. Once they feel they have adequately done so, they turn their attention to what they anticipate next. The sequence of questions above demonstrates a useful strategy with notetaking. The interviewer addressed a critical issue (the last time Mark spoke with the victim) in an indirect, nonthreatening way. He then moved the questioning into an area that was comfortable for the interviewee. Once the interviewee's attention was directed to another topic, the interviewer then brought the questioning back to the critical issue. Using notetaking as a way of returning to important themes allows you to subtly control the direction and pace of the interview. In addition, it can help you explore critical issues in detail in ways that are not challenging or threatening. Remember that the interview is about detailed information gathering that serves many purposes in supporting an ongoing investigation.

As previously discussed, within the interview setting (particularly early in the interview), oblivious narcissists may appear cooperative and willing to talk to you. Keep in mind that they typically portray this cooperative attitude because it is advantageous to them. In many instances they are as interested in finding out what you know as you are in gathering information from them. They may even ask questions to obtain information. For example,

Mr. Thompson: Do you think something bad has happened to her?
Interviewer: I don't like to form any opinions or speculate before I have had the chance to gather all the facts. Especially in these types of cases where there could be any number of explanations. Now, back to …

—or—

Mr. Thompson: *Have you found out anything helpful?*
Interviewer: I'm really still gathering information right now, and I haven't had a chance to sort it out yet. Anyway, back to …

Finally, we need to emphasize a point previously discussed. It is critically important to resist showing whatever negative emotions (e.g., anger, defensiveness, frustration, boredom) you might experience and to resist acting on any urge to challenge or confront the interviewee. Approaching and conducting the interview in ways discussed within this section decrease the chances of the oblivious narcissist provoking you to respond negatively. However, be prepared for dismissive or condescending behavior, particularly when you move into substantive issues. Even in the absence of such behavior, constantly placing yourself in the "one-down" position with the oblivious narcissist requires a lot of patience and emotional control. It is equally important to resist showing—verbally or nonverbally—any positive feelings and emotions (e.g., satisfaction or smugness) that give the appearance of a change in the power differential. If you allow yourself to let these emotions get the best of you, it will interfere with your ability to be effective and could potentially shut down the interview.

Key Points to Remember

Do

- Do be patient.
- Do treat them special.
- Do be attentive and responsive to their needs.
- Do allow them perceived control.
- DO act deferentially.
- Do give them personal space.

Don't

- Don't devalue, minimize, or condescend.
- Don't threaten their identity (by being confrontational or placing yourself in a position of superiority).
- Don't do anything to threaten their sense of superiority or grandiosity.
- Don't let your emotions show (positive or negative).
- Don't take it personally.
- Don't invade their personal space.
- Don't be overly friendly.
- Don't do or say things that imply closeness or intimacy.

The Vulnerable Narcissist

Josh was getting ready for school when there was a knock on the door and his mother said, "We have company coming tonight so I need you to come home right after school so you're here to help out."

"No problem, Mom," he said. "I'll be here." Josh grabbed his bag and ran out of the house toward the bus stop. He got on the bus and looked for a seat, trying to avoid sitting by the typical "bullies" or "popular" kids. Josh did not have a lot of friends, nor was he involved in many school activities. He had one or two close friends but other than that, he kept to himself because he felt that no one really understood him anyway. Josh found a seat, opened up his notebook, and began writing.

The bus pulled up to the school entrance and Josh got off. He headed toward his locker, enduring the sideways glances and degrading remarks as he passed by the jocks, the brainiacs, and various other cliques. Eventually, he saw a couple of his friends (guys who seemed to be as unaccepted as he was) and walked over. He approached them, shaking his head and muttered, "These idiots, always thinking they're so much better than everyone else and they're not. We'll see who's laughing after the basketball game on Friday." The conversation changed to something else and Josh knelt down to put his books in his locker. He grabbed what he needed for his first class and shut his locker. He told the guys he would see them later and walked off, not noticing that he had left his notebook on the floor.

Another student overheard this conversation and saw Josh's notebook on the floor. He picked it up and looked through it. After glancing at some of the writings, he took the notebook to the principal and told him about Josh's remarks. After listening to the student and looking through the notebook, the principal immediately activated the school's threat assessment protocol, which included talking with some of Josh's teachers. His English teacher, Mr. Edwards, was called into the office and briefed on the situation. As the principal handed him the notebook to look through, he said, "What he writes seems to go from one extreme to the other. In some entries he seems very depressed and writes about how much pain he is in and how worthless he feels. Other entries are filled with anger and threats directed at the world in general for not realizing what a sensitive and creative person he is. In some cases he goes from one extreme to the other in the same essay."

Mr. Edwards did not quite know what to make of the writings. Josh was a quiet and polite student who never caused any trouble, a shy kid who rarely said anything and who stayed in the background. As Mr. Edwards put it, "You would hardly even notice him in class. I don't ever call on him because he seems so uncomfortable if attention is drawn to him."

Josh was brought in for questioning because of concern over the threatening content of his writings.

___

Description of the Vulnerable Narcissist

The beginning of this chapter discussed the fact that vulnerable and oblivious narcissism both begin as the creation of a self-image that protects the person from the demands of day-to-day reality. But these two narcissistic styles accomplish their protective functions in quite different ways. For the oblivious narcissist, the created self-image is a grandiose and powerful one that ignores any suggestions to the contrary. For the vulnerable narcissist, the self-image is a thin-skinned and sensitive one in a world that does not make allowances for the person's exquisite creativity.

It is easy to understand how oblivious narcissism works, and the arrogant and exhibitionistic behavior that characterizes that part of the narcissistic spectrum is usually quite obvious. Vulnerable narcissism is more subtle, involving a self-concept based on unappreciated sensitivity in individuals who stay out of the limelight and are vigilant to perceived slights. Perhaps the best way to understand the differences between oblivious and vulnerable narcissism is to look at Figure 2.1.

In this figure, the vulnerable end of the continuum represents the origination of narcissism. The top circle represents the self-image

The greater the gap between the grandiose self-image (fantasy) and reality, the greater the level of internal conflict and anxiety; and the greater the fluctuation in self-esteem.

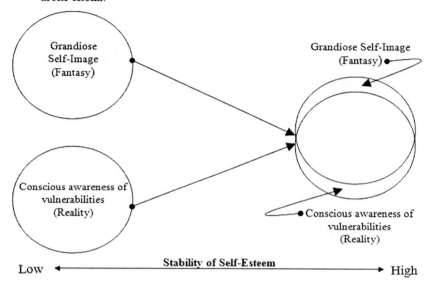

Figure 2.1   The narcissistic continuum. The greater the gap between the grandiose self-Image (fantasy) and reality, the greater the level of Internal conflict and anxiety; and the greater the fluctuation in self-esteem.

that the individual creates as an escape from the demands of reality, represented by the bottom circle. The critical differentiating feature between vulnerable and oblivious narcissism is the gap between the created self-image and reality. Oblivious narcissists have managed to mostly eliminate that gap, fusing the two worlds so that fantasy has, in essence, become their reality. For vulnerable narcissists, however, the two worlds remain separated. The creation of the sensitive and misunderstood person they desire to be provides temporary relief from feelings of inadequacy, but reality impinges endlessly. This gap between fantasy and reality is where every slight and perceived injustice is cataloged, where anger and resentment seethe, where anxiety and hypervigilance are always present, and where feelings of self-worth are in constant fluctuation.

Although vulnerable narcissists might wish to receive the admiration and respect that their delicately creative talent should bring, they actively avoid anything that could draw attention to themselves because they are terrified of exposing the weakness of their reality. The result is a vigilant, fragile, and inhibited personality structure. The vulnerable narcissist bases his sense of being special not on a grandiose and powerful self-image, but rather on one emphasizing fragility and sensitivity. It is important to note that feeling special does not necessarily mean that you see yourself as better than others; it just means you feel that you are different in ways that others should appreciate. For vulnerably narcissistic individuals, what is different about them is that they see themselves as more sensitive, more delicate, and more thin-skinned than others. Endlessly vigilant to indications that others are not making appropriate allowances for those differences, the vulnerable narcissist lives in a chronic state of resentment. They quietly keep track and ruminate over every perceived slight, while their anger boils just under the surface.

In summary, vulnerably narcissistic individuals are acutely aware of their weaknesses and construct a protective self-concept as sensitive, fragile, and unappreciated. Therefore:

- They actively avoid anything that might draw attention to themselves because they are terrified of having their vulnerabilities exposed
- They often appear quiet, shy, inhibited, and unassuming
- They escape into a self-concept of exquisite sensitivity to protect against feelings of inadequacy
- Within this concept of self as different because of special sensitivity, they believe they should be treated with great care and respect
- They continually monitor every situation for even the slightest indication that this care and respect is not forthcoming
- They can vacillate between internally and externally aggressive thoughts

Assessing the Vulnerable Narcissist

This section is not designed to exhaust all the sources of information you might use to conduct an indirect assessment of a potential interviewee. Rather, it is designed to present a number of questions that address the core features of vulnerable narcissism and offer some suggestions regarding sources of information typically useful in answering those questions. Remember that narcissistic features exist on a continuum. These questions are not for the purpose of diagnosing the interviewee with Narcissistic Personality Disorder, but rather for determining the presence and strength of vulnerably narcissistic features. For convenience, this section is written referencing a male interviewee, but the suggestions are equally relevant for women.

Not only is vulnerable narcissism more complex psychologically, but it can also be more difficult to assess. This is because grandiosity is not the driving force behind the behavior of the vulnerable narcissist. Instead, burdened by feelings of low self-worth, the person presents an introverted image while the narcissistic features express themselves in subtle and indirect ways.

One area in which these features manifest is within intimate relationships. When talking to current or former intimate partners, try to determine

- Would intimate partners describe the relationship as lacking in intimacy or emotional closeness? Would they describe his behaviors within the relationship as sullen, demanding, or vindictive? Does he make his partner feel that she is there to appreciate his sensitivity?
- Is he indifferent to the needs and feelings of his partner?
- Does he feel that his partner does not fully understand how thin-skinned he is?
- When he feels his needs are not being met, does he tend to retaliate by withdrawing and becoming quietly angry?

In most other areas of his life, the vulnerable narcissist tends to behave in avoidant ways in order to reduce the risk of being rejected, humiliated, or shamed. Family members, friends, coworkers, and classmates can provide information regarding these behaviors, as well as thoughts and feelings he might be experiencing. Ask them

- Does he avoid actively participating in school activities or social events?
- Was he ever bullied, teased, or ostracized by his peers?
- Would others describe him as quiet or shy?
- Would they consider him a "loner"?
- Would others describe him as odd or different?
- Does he tend to stay in the background?
- Does he have any close friends? If so, does he confide in them?
- Would friends say that he tends to get depressed?
- Does he hold grudges against others?
- Does he keep track of the ways in which he thinks he has been mistreated?
- Does he talk about being misunderstood or about others making him feel bad?
- Has he ever expressed thoughts of self-harm?
- Has he ever expressed thoughts of aggression toward others?

Particularly with late teens or young adults, a good place to look for indications of internalizing (e.g., depression, suicidal) and externalizing (e.g., aggression toward others) thoughts and feelings is through personal writings. Look for the following:

- Does he keep a journal or diary?
- Are there any personal writings (e.g., letters, class essays, notebooks) that give insight into his thoughts and feelings?
- Do the writings reflect thoughts and feelings that are internalizing (e.g., depression, suicidal) or externalizing (e.g., aggression toward others)?

Within the work environment, the vulnerable narcissist tends to follow the avoidant pattern of behavior. However, he may also behave in ways that reflect his feelings of "specialness." When talking to coworkers or others he may work with, remember to find out the following:

- Does he have a job that requires little interaction with other people?

- Does he have a history of avoiding or turning down promotions or positions that would require him to interact more with others (managerial responsibilities)?
- Does he complain or has he filed complaints about his needs not being accommodated?

Preparation Issues

Preparation is a critical aspect of any interview. This section is intended to provide you with an understanding of issues that are important as you prepare to interview the vulnerable narcissist.

Understanding Your Reactions to the Individual

Before the actual interview begins, you need to be keenly aware of the ways in which you are likely to instinctively respond to the interviewee. Being the complex disorder that it is, the vulnerably narcissistic individual can present in a variety of ways. For those who initially present as "people pleasing," be careful not to misinterpret their behavior and demeanor as being cooperative. Some may present themselves as self-effacing, giving the impression that they are critical of themselves. With these individuals, avoid the temptation to rescue or protect. There are also those who may seem more reserved or withdrawn. It is much more difficult to get those individuals to participate in the interview because they show little emotion and are more wary of what is going on. Because they tend to give you very little to work with, it is easy to become frustrated or to want to give up on the interview. Vulnerable narcissists can also present as angry and self-righteous, engaging in sarcastic, passive-aggressive behaviors. This can become problematic because it is natural to react in a contentious manner. In all these instances, it is essential that you take your time, working to maintain a calm, supportive environment.

Who Should Conduct the Interview

Understanding the vulnerably narcissistic individual and what you are likely to encounter is critical to conducting an effective interview. It is equally critical that you possess the right combination of personality traits, given the information we have presented in order to have the best chance of a successful outcome.

The vulnerable narcissist presents some unique challenges to the interviewer. At any given moment, these individuals may take refuge in the self-concept of exquisite sensitivity they have created, delicately navigating a reality in which they are acutely aware of their weaknesses; turning on themselves in shame, humiliation, and hopelessness when they feel their inadequacies have been exposed, or blaming others for not recognizing how special they are and for making them feel so inadequate. Therefore, patience, calmness, and accurate empathy are all crucial for the interview. Patience is necessary because these are individuals who believe that other people do not care or are indifferent to who they are or what their needs might be. So, at best, they are going to be wary of any attempts by the interviewer to show interest in them. It takes time to get through to these individuals, given their fragile and volatile personality structure. Underneath the surface is resentment from a lifetime of unresolved anger over the slights, criticisms, or injustices they have collected. The combination of these features, along with their tendency to harbor grudges, makes time and patience critical in order for the interviewer to navigate what is a virtual mine field. In addition, their deep desire for someone to understand what is so unique and special about them requires the ability on the part of the interviewer to maintain a reassuring and empathic demeanor. Calmness and empathy are essential when interviewing narcissistic individuals because they have spent a lifetime scanning for any potential threat to their self-esteem. They are adept at spotting whether or not someone is genuinely concerned, and you should not underestimate their ability to read your true emotions.

The age and gender of the interviewer is generally of less importance than the calmness and empathy described above. However, age or gender issues could be relevant for a specific interviewee. For example, in the vignette of Josh, the interviewer should probably be someone old enough to be his mother or father. At the core of vulnerable narcissism is a sense of inadequacy. In the case of Josh, that inadequacy is particularly heightened around peers, and a young, "hip" interviewer might be fear-provoking for him. So, an older interviewer who projects calmness, reassurance, and understanding would have a better chance of creating a safe, nonthreatening environment.

As always, a thoughtful self-evaluation on the part of the interviewer is important. Typically, the law enforcement officer who is assigned the case is likely to conduct the interview. If, however, it is determined that someone else would be better suited, that determination should take precedence in order to increase the likelihood of the interview's success.

Number of Interviewers

Because of their extreme sensitivity, vulnerably narcissistic individuals believe they are special and different, incapable of being understood by others. However, they secretly desire to be appreciated and for their sensitivity to be recognized. When others fail to do so (as they inevitably will), vulnerably narcissistic individuals circumvent further damage to their self-image by convincing themselves that others are indifferent to their special needs or just do not care. One interviewer has a better chance of creating an environment in which he or she is perceived by the interviewee as attentive, concerned, and willing to listen. If you must have two interviewers in the room, then it would be best to have the second one somewhat removed, but still within sight so as not to increase suspiciousness or anxiety. He or she should take notes and make sure not to interrupt.

Physical Space/Environment/Interpersonal Space

With the vulnerable narcissist, the location of the interview is less important than the physical space itself. If it is to take place in a law enforcement facility, try to find a location that is more warm and friendly than the typical stark interview or interrogation room. We would recommend a smaller office or conference room, if at all possible. If you have to resort to the more standard setting, then be sure to turn off all phones and minimize any distractions. Make every effort to provide interviewees with the space they desire by sitting well separated from them but not with a complete physical barrier. This may sound like a slight distinction, but it is the nuances that can make or break an interview. Always try to maximize their comfort to help minimize their level of anxiety. Something as simple as having several chairs available can be a good way to start the interview. For example, when offering vulnerably narcissistic interviewees a seat, you might say, "We have lots of chairs, so pick whichever seems most comfortable to you." By inviting them in and giving them the option of where to sit, you are helping to create a less threatening environment. Vulnerably narcissistic people are often socially awkward and anxious. Because they are insecure, you want to make sure not to impinge on their personal space.

Nonverbal Behavior

With the vulnerable narcissist, it is as much about your nonverbal behavior as it is about the questions that you ask. Your body language should coincide with what you say in order to create an environment similar to that of a conversation between friends. Imagine how you would be if you were listening to a good friend telling you about his or her troubles. The empathy, attentiveness, and interest that you would show is what you want to reflect in your nonverbal behavior.

Questions

Vulnerable narcissists are much like paranoid individuals in that they continually look for anything in their environment that they can interpret as threatening. Therefore, questions should be open-ended but structured in a very straightforward manner. Avoid unclear, compound, or complex questions. In addition, we cannot overemphasize the importance of the background and biographical phase of this interview. This is the phase in which you can utilize prepared questions that subtly explore the areas outlined above.

Recording the Interview (Notetaking, Audio/Video Recording)

We would recommend that the interviewer not take notes but rather rely on audio or video recording, because it will allow the interviewee to feel that the interviewer is solely focused on him. If the interviewer needs to take notes, then it needs to be continuous and not just utilized at times when the interviewer feels the information is important. Remember that vulnerably narcissistic individuals are extraordinarily attuned to every nuance in the environment. If a second interviewer is going to be present, then it would be beneficial to have him or her take the notes so that the primary interviewer can give full attention to the interviewee.

Time Frame

It is important that you slowly ease into the interview, taking a considerable amount of time during the background and biographical information-gathering phase. The actual interview phase should also proceed at a relatively easy pace. For vulnerable narcissists, it is critical that you avoid provoking the kinds of negative responses (e.g., anxiety, anger) that they are prone to experiencing. This is best achieved by a deliberate, calm, and empathic tone and pace.

The Interview

Now that you have a good understanding of the behaviors that vulnerably narcissistic individuals are likely to engage in during the interview process and the reasons for those behaviors, settled on an effective interview style, and engaged in thorough preparation, it is time for the actual interview. This section cannot be a comprehensive discussion of everything you may encounter, but it will address many of the details that increase the likelihood of the interview going well. In this section we use the vulnerably narcissistic vignette of Josh presented earlier to emphasize key points made throughout this section.

Interviews with Josh's teachers and a review of his writings suggest that his self-esteem is poor and that he feels that no one realizes how sensitive he is. Therefore, you should begin the interview by inquiring about immediate needs. For example,

Interviewer: Hi Josh. Before we get started, can I get you something to drink or something to snack on while we talk? The men's room is down the hall. We have a bunch of chairs, so feel free to choose whichever looks most comfortable.

Beginning the interview in this way sets an immediate tone of care and concern. Once the interview begins, you want to be fully attentive, interested in everything the interviewee has to say. In addition, minimize distractions or interruptions that would take the focus off the interviewee. However, you can interrupt from time to time to focus on the interviewee's needs by asking if he would like to take a break, use the restroom, or have another soda or snack. This accommodating approach subtly lets him know that you "get" his sensitivity, that you understand that he is different, and that you can respect him for who he is.

You want to ease into the interview, avoiding language that is critical or accusatory. Vulnerably narcissistic individuals are incredibly sensitive to anything that they interpret as a threat to their self-esteem. Therefore, the early stages of the interview should be about reducing anxiety and setting a conversational tone. Think of it as creating an environment that is more of a mutual conversation than an interview. For example,

Interviewer: Josh, I'd like to talk with you about some of the things you've written and said to your friends.

Conveying empathy is an important aspect of the interview, but be careful about the manner in which you do it. Vulnerably narcissistic people often feel as if they are different in a unique way, and they vacillate between wanting others to understand how they feel and believing that they cannot. Therefore, you want to avoid empathic statements such as "I understand how you feel" or "I know how you must feel." Instead, convey empathy through your demeanor and by reflecting statements back to the interviewee. For example,

Josh: You don't know the crap I have to constantly deal with from the kids at school.
Interviewer: It seems you feel that other people have caused you a lot of pain.

—or—

Interviewer: It seems you feel like nobody cares about you.

Conveying empathy in this way indicates that you "get" that he is different, while letting him preserve his sense of uniqueness. Using the right empathic language (e.g., "It seems like" or "It sounds like") avoids provoking responses (either verbally or in thought) such as, "How do you know how I feel?" or "You have no idea how I feel." In addition, reflecting statements back to the interviewee indicates that you are listening to what he is saying and can facilitate communication.

The following writing showed up in Josh's notebook:

> But now it's time to pay…
> They are the ones who are pathetic and weak.
> They are the ones who don't get it.

This gives us some insight into the bind he is in and how he copes with it. While the vulnerable side of this individual constantly struggles with poor self-esteem that makes him feel "pathetic and weak," his narcissistic defenses externalize the blame onto others for "causing" him to feel that way. As an interviewer, you are always walking a fine line between validating his sense of victimization and running the risk of stirring up feelings of vulnerability. For example,

Interviewer: It seems like other people have tried to make you feel like less than you are, *or* it seems like other kids at school act like they are better than you.

If at some point you do or say something that upsets the interviewee, do not be afraid to apologize. For example,

Interviewer: You felt humiliated.
Josh: Don't tell me how I felt. You have no idea how I feel.
Interviewer: You're right. I'm sorry, and I guess I'd get pissed if somebody tried to tell me how I felt about something. I'd appreciate it if you'd tell me how you felt when they said that to you.

By apologizing, you are addressing the interviewee's perception that others do not understand. However, the apology also counters that perception by letting him know that you recognize it and are not afraid to engage it. In addition, you are letting him know that you are not perfect, that you can acknowledge your own reactions and short-comings, and that you can try to see things from the interviewee's viewpoint.

This section focuses on the sensitivity and vulnerability of these individuals. However, remember that there is also a narcissistic side to them. Therefore, you must be prepared for those occasions when that aspect of their personality may emerge during the interview.

Key Points to Remember

Do

- Do take time to make interviewees comfortable within the setting.
- Do attend to immediate needs.
- Do listen attentively.
- Do use empathic language, but be careful how you use it.

Don't

- Don't tell them you know how they feel or that you understand how they feel.
- Don't act in superior manner.
- Don't threaten their sense of comfort.
- Don't react defensively or punitively to their behavior.

References

American Psychiatric Association. (2000). *Diagnostic and statistical manual of mental disorders (4th ed., text rev.)*. Washington, DC: American Psychiatric Association.

Beck, A., Freeman, A., and Davis, D. (2007). *Cognitive therapy of personality disorders (2nd ed.)*. New York, NY: Guilford Publications, Inc.

Gabbard, G. O. (1989). Two subtypes of narcissistic personality disorder. *Bulletin of the Menninger Clinic*, 53, 527–532.

3
THE ANTISOCIAL PERSONALITY

Michael arrived at the office after having been called in to see his probation officer again.

"Do you know why I called you in again?" Mr. Jones asked.

"I have no idea," Michael replied.

"We've got another positive test," said Mr. Jones.

Michael shrugged and said, "Well, it must be wrong. You guys must have screwed up somewhere cause it ain't me."

"Michael, this is the third time you've failed a drug test in the past month."

"Well, what am I supposed to do?" Michael asked. "No one will give me a job. Every time I get out of prison, they tell me to get a job but no one will ever hire me because I have a criminal record or I'm not qualified. Besides, I've got too much class to be working some minimum-wage job."

"But Mike, you don't have the skills to do anything else. You never finished high school or even attended any of the vocational training that I set up for you."

"Why would I when I can make more money in one night selling dope than I can make in five months working in some fast food restaurant?"

Irritated, Mr. Jones said, "Yeah, Michael, you can make more money selling dope, but it's wrong. It's illegal. And you'll just end up back in jail, or worse. You could get yourself killed. You haven't even looked for a job –"

Michael interrupted, "What does it matter? I'm never gonna get a fair break! The only way to get what I want is to take it. That's what everybody does anyway, right?"

Mr. Jones replied, "All you ever do is make excuses and blame everyone else for the problems you bring on yourself. You know, you tell me that no one will hire you when the fact is that you've never even looked for a job. I followed up with some of the places where you said you put in an application and you haven't even applied. You just continually lie. You lie to me and everyone else. You haven't been able to hold a job. The last time you had a job was for only two weeks."

"Well, I couldn't work for that guy. He was harassing me."

"Michael, you've been in and out of jail since you were thirteen years old. Let's just take a look here at your history: assault with a deadly weapon, armed robbery, burglary, DUI, multiple drug offenses. And all I hear from you is that it's not your fault. At what point are you going to take responsibility for the things that you've done?"

"Look, I know I've screwed up, but I can't go back to jail. You gotta help me out here. This is going to kill my mother. That's why I even got involved in selling drugs in the first place—to help her out. I don't want her to have to work so hard." Tears started to well up in his eyes and he went on to say, "She can't make it on her social security and I wanted her to have something since she raised me and my brothers and sisters by herself. You've gotta help me out here," he pleaded. "I promise. I'll do whatever I have to do."

When Michael got back from meeting with his parole officer, his girlfriend was at the apartment. She immediately jumped all over him because she was upset that he hadn't found a job, hadn't contributed any money toward the baby on the way, and convinced he was still seeing an ex-girlfriend of his. Already stressed out from the meeting, he didn't react well and they both got physically aggressive. She shouted at him, and he responded by shoving her and calling her a bitch. Then he slammed the door and left the apartment.

He called a few friends to meet him at a nearby bar to have a drink. The bar was crowded and it was getting tough to move. The guy standing next to him bumped into him and Michael shot him a look. His friends entered the bar and Michael nodded to them from where he was. As they made their way toward him, the guy bumped Michael again. They exchanged words and it quickly escalated. They decided to take it outside and their friends all followed. A fight broke out, shots were fired, and the man who was arguing with Michael fell to the ground. Although no one saw who fired the gun, a witness saw three men jump into a car and speed out of the parking lot. The license plate that was reported to the police came back registered to Michael.

Description of the Antisocial Personality

In describing Antisocial Personality Disorder (ASPD), the *Diagnostic and Statistical Manual of Mental Disorders* ([DSM-IV-TR]; American Psychiatric Association, 2000) draws a picture of impulsive, irresponsible, and often aggressive behavior, apparent by early adolescence and noteworthy for a disregard for rules, laws, and the rights of others. Understanding the core features of the antisocial personality—a sense of entitlement, deceit and manipulation, lack of impulse control, aggressive irritability, low frustration tolerance, externalization of blame, and rationalization—will help in preparing for the challenges these individuals present during interviews.

For antisocial individuals, their sense of entitlement leads to the attitude of "I deserve it," their lack of impulse control says, "I want it now" (immediate gratification), and their aggressive temperament says, "I'm going to take it," thus satisfying that need. When things go wrong, it is never their fault, and their externalization of blame can at times seem almost surreal. They view the world as one in which rules and laws keep them from achieving what they are entitled to and, therefore, they endlessly lie or bend the truth, manipulate others, and violate whatever rules and laws are necessary to serve their own needs. True antisocial individuals are perpetually in this cycle of feeling entitled, having aggressive urges, acting out on those urges, and then rationalizing why they did it.

While antisocial individuals clearly engage in acting-out behaviors, both criminal and noncriminal, typically, most are not violent people. When they do engage in violence, it tends to be impulsive rather than planned or predatory in nature, and often coexists with alcohol or illegal substance use. Further, the impulsive violence they engage in tends to be driven by emotion (e.g., jealousy, anger, frustration) and lacks the cold and callous quality that is characteristic of psychopathic violence.

Due to their low levels of self-discipline (the ability to force themselves to do the things they should do) and impulse control (the ability to stop themselves from doing things they should not do), antisocial personalities tend to underachieve in most aspects of their lives. They typically do not obtain high levels of education, sustain stable employment, or maintain long-term relationships. As a result, they often spend their lives in and out of relationships and jobs, and, for many, correctional facilities as well.

Antisocial individuals can be personable and likeable when they are not under stress or threat. However, their ability to form close emotional connections with others is limited, so even those "close to them" can be victimized by their aggressive, impulsive behaviors. That is not to say that they cannot maintain some loyalty or feel some level of guilt or remorse. Guilt and remorse, like many other traits, exist on a continuum and need to be evaluated on an individual basis.

In summary, antisocial individuals:

- Possess a low level of impulse control (the ability to stop themselves from doing things they should not do)
- Possess a low level of self-discipline (the ability to force themselves to do the things they should do)
- Possess a low tolerance for frustration
- Exhibit poor emotional control (particularly anger)
- Tend to react aggressively to stress and frustration
- Tend to have a sense of entitlement
- Tend to view rules, laws, and the rights of others as obstacles to that entitlement
- Continually bend or break rules, laws, and the rights of others for their own needs
- Tend to be deceitful and manipulative
- Tend not to be dependable or reliable
- Tend to have difficulty maintaining long-term relationships

- Tend to have difficulty sustaining stable employment
- Tend to rationalize and/or externalize blame for their actions and failures
- Possess a limited ability to feel empathy
- Possess a limited ability to maintain loyalty
- Exhibit this behavior since early adolescence

Assessing the Antisocial Personality

This section is not designed to exhaust all sources of information you may utilize to conduct an indirect assessment of a potential interviewee. Rather, it is designed to suggest a number of questions that address the core features of the antisocial personality and offer some suggestions regarding sources of information typically useful in answering those questions. Antisocial features exist on a continuum. These questions are not for the purpose of diagnosing the interviewee with ASPD, but rather for determining the presence and intensity of antisocial features. Clinically, ASPD is more frequently diagnosed in men (American Psychiatric Association, 2000), and we have used masculine pronouns in describing the assessment of this personality.

Antisocial individuals have much in common with individuals with narcissistic, borderline, and psychopathic personalities. More often than not, the characteristics of antisocial personality overlap with at least one of these other personalities. The questions we are suggesting will help in identifying the antisocial aspects of what is often a complex picture. This section is divided into three subsections: important areas and nature of inquiry, questions to answer, and relevant sources of information.

Important Areas and Nature of Inquiry

For an accurate assessment of antisocial features, the questions should address the areas in this subsection. It is important to be as specific as possible. For example, it is not enough to know that the person has a history of aggressive behavior; you must go on to ask whether those behaviors seem impulsive and poorly planned. Behavior that is more calculating, deliberate, and predatory may indicate the presence of psychopathy. Therefore, when evaluating information in the following areas, look for the core features of the antisocial personality: impulsivity, irresponsibility, poor tolerance for frustration, and stress.

- History and nature of acting out behaviors (criminal and non-criminal) (impulsive, aggressive, reckless)
- History and nature of violent behaviors (impulsive, relational, drug/alcohol involvement)
- History and nature of relationships (number and duration, stability, abuse issues)
- History and nature of employment (stability, skill level, disciplinary issues)
- Level of education and relevant issues (truancy, problem behaviors)
- Family of origin information (stability of childhood environment, presence of abuse, lack of emotional closeness, presence of antisocial traits or other mental health issues in parents or siblings)
- Traits and characteristics (impulsivity; issues with anger, depression, anxiety; stress tolerance; ability to form some level of close emotional bonds; ability to feel some level of remorse or guilt)
- Substance use/abuse history

Questions

The following questions are not meant to be inclusive, but rather to provide examples that can flesh out some of the topics listed above:

- Since the age of fifteen, does the person have a criminal history or clear acting-out behaviors that have either not come to the attention of law enforcement or have not resulted in arrests/convictions (e.g., fighting or other aggressive behaviors, excessive gambling, domestic violence, drug or alcohol abuse)? This question asks about a pervasive and longstanding pattern of behavior indicating impulsivity, irresponsibility, and a violation of the rights of others.

- Does the history of criminal or acting out behavior involve violence? If so, is it affective violence? That is, violence that is impulsive and emotionally based (e.g., jealousy, anger), as opposed to calculating, predatory violence. Not all antisocial individuals are violent; but if there is violence, it tends to be impulsive in nature.
- Does he have a history of unstable relationships? Because of anger, impulsivity, and control issues, relationships tend to be volatile. In addition, emotional connections are typically shallow, resulting in a history of multiple relationships.
- What is the person's educational history? Because of their lack of self-discipline, conflict with authority, and proneness to boredom, antisocial individuals tend not to achieve high levels of education.
- Does he have an unstable employment history? Because of lack of impulse control and self-discipline and the likelihood of ongoing conflict with authority, work histories tend to be erratic.
- What was his family life like growing up? Antisocial individuals often come from childhood environments that were unstable (lack of emotional closeness, abuse/neglect, alcohol/substance use within the home, other family members with antisocial traits or other mental health issues). ASPD occurs more frequently in the first-degree biological relatives of those with this disorder (American Psychiatric Association, 2000).
- Has he demonstrated the ability to form a close emotional bond with anyone? Antisocial individuals show some limited capacity to form bonds with others.
- How does he respond after acting aggressively toward someone? Antisocial individuals show some limited capacity to feel remorse or guilt, a characteristic that differentiates them from psychopathic individuals.
- How does he respond in stressful situations? Because of their low-frustration tolerance and impulsivity, antisocial individuals tend to respond with anger and aggression.
- Does he have a history of alcohol/illegal substance use/abuse, a common finding in antisocial individuals?

- Has he been previously diagnosed with antisocial personality disorder or antisocial traits? Because of their likely involvement with the criminal justice system, many of these individuals may have had court-ordered psychological evaluations. These evaluations may be part of case files from previous offenses, and often provide a wealth of information.

Sources of Information

Because the antisocial personality involves impulsive, irresponsible, and often aggressive behavior extending back to childhood or adolescence, these individuals frequently compile extensive amounts of collateral information The following sources of information are often productive:

- Collateral interviews (e.g., former and current intimate partners, family members, friends, and coworkers)
- Adult and juvenile criminal records/case files
- Educational records
- Financial records
- DMV records
- Employment records
- Mental health records

Preparation Issues

Preparation is a critical aspect of any interview. This section is intended to provide you with an understanding of those issues that are important considerations as you prepare to interview the antisocial individual.

Understanding Your Reactions to the Individual

Before conducting the interview, it is important to be keenly aware of the instinctive ways in which you are likely to respond to the antisocial personality. A common reaction that interviewers have with antisocial individuals is one in which they conclude that "He's not really that bad a guy" or "Maybe he didn't really mean to do it." Many antisocial people come off as likeable in interpersonal settings, and they are often very good at putting others at ease. They read people well, quickly spot vulnerabilities, and use those vulnerabilities to their benefit. When you find yourself feeling sorry for the individual, you should evaluate your reaction carefully in relation to the factual details of the case and the context in which you are doing the interview.

With antisocial individuals, you may also feel as if you are establishing a bond during the interview process. However, it is important to remember that they have a limited capacity for emotional attachment, and any feelings of rapport are likely a manipulation on their part.

Who Should Conduct the Interview

Understanding the antisocial individual and what you are likely to encounter is critical to conducting an effective interview. It is equally critical that you possess the right combination of personality traits, given the information we have presented, in order to have the best chance of a successful outcome.

If possible, you should choose an interviewer who has substantial experience working with antisocial individuals. Ideally, the interviewer would be someone who simply, through his or her appearance and demeanor, communicates competence, experience, and authority, tempered with a sense of nonjudgmental fairness. You do not want someone who needs to engage competitively in order to exert control of the interview. What you are seeking is that person in your department who represents authority without being overtly authoritative and who has a flair for engaging individuals in a more conversational way.

All of this is important because it is that combination of quiet confidence and of being in control, to which the antisocial individual can relate. The key to the antisocial interview is establishing the sense that you know what you are doing, you are good at what you do, and you are sincere in terms of wanting to help. That becomes even more critical as the severity of the offense increases. When the consequences are greatest and antisocial individuals realize that they cannot get out of their predicament, they seem to recognize that they have no one else to turn to. Ironically, although they are not people of their word, what they are looking for in you is someone who is true to his or her word. Therefore, they need just that someone who is straightforward, professional, and competent.

An important consideration for the interview is the age and number of interviewers. As suggested, one interviewer meeting the above criteria is optimal. However, if you have two people in on the interview, make sure that one of them is older and experienced, competent, and genuine. Then pair that individual with a younger interviewer who serves to bolster the credibility of the older interviewer and assures the interviewee that "Hey, he means what he says."

For the antisocial individual, the gender of the interviewer is not as great a consideration as the age of the interviewer and the qualities that he or she possesses. Younger interviewers can be effective if they demonstrate the qualities of confidence, sincerity, and competence that usually come with age and experience. Whether it is a male or female interviewer, we would strongly suggest an older individual whose competence and abilities are apparent, yet subdued.

As always, an honest self-evaluation on the part of the interviewer is crucial. Typically, the law enforcement officer who is assigned the case is likely to conduct the interview. If, however, after an objective self-evaluation it is determined that someone else would be better suited, the success of the interview should take priority.

Number of Interviewers

As mentioned above, with the antisocial individual, we recommend one interviewer if at all possible. The chance of establishing any true sense of rapport is unlikely; however, you can establish an environment in which the interviewee may be receptive to an alliance with you that he or she finds self-serving. You have a better chance of creating this environment in a one-on-one setting.

Physical Space/Environment/Interpersonal Space

For the antisocial individual, the location of the interview has much less impact on the outcome than with some of the other personalities discussed in this book. With regard to interpersonal space, we recommend maintaining a professional distance during the interview of an antisocial individual. Moving into an interviewee's personal space is typically done to convey empathy, build rapport, or increase anxiety—none of which are particularly useful with antisocial individuals. As previously stated, you are not likely to be successful in developing any real rapport with antisocial individuals, and increasing anxiety or any other negative emotion is likely to shut down the interview.

Nonverbal Behavior

The interviewer must be careful not to underestimate the perceptual abilities of antisocial individuals. These are often individuals skilled at spotting vulnerabilities and very much in tune with expressions and emotions. They can quickly pick up on even subtle indications that the interviewer is being judgmental, disbelieving, disdainful, superior, accusatory, angry, frustrated, or irritated. Therefore, you have to be very careful not to allow those sorts of feelings to manifest themselves. Along those same lines, you must be equally concerned with conveying certain things like genuineness, sincerity, concern, and friendliness through your nonverbal behavior. For example, place yourself at the interviewee's level, lean forward to show interest, and maintain open body language. The amount of eye contact should be determined in relation to the level of hostility, aggression, and uncooperativeness of the interviewee. The more hostile, aggressive, and uncooperative the interviewee, the more likely he or she is to interpret prolonged eye contact as adversarial. For those who do not display those attitudes, prolonged eye contact is acceptable as long as it is within the context of the conversation. However, in any case, you usually want to avoid prolonged eye contact during extended silences.

Questions

With the antisocial individual, we suggest a combination of straightforward questions and more open-ended ones that elicit lengthier, more explanatory responses. This is useful in both the background and biographical information phase as well as the substantive part of the interview. During the first phase, closed-ended questions are necessary in gathering specific information. However, open-ended questions are very useful in extending this phase, which allows you to establish a comfortable interviewing style and to explore issues that may provide important information regarding topics to follow up on during the substantive phase of the interview. Closed-ended questions during the substantive phase should be used to verify and clarify answers. However, it is often best not to interrupt the person's answers to open-ended questions with closed-ended questions or statements.

Recording the Interview (Notetaking, Audio/Video Recording)

Audio or video recording is strongly recommended for any interview with an antisocial individual. Notetaking is recommended with the antisocial individual even with the presence of audio or video recording and critical in the absence of any other form of recording the interview. There is a tendency for antisocial individuals to be inconsistent in their explanations of their behavior. Therefore, it is important to capture those inconsistencies for use as the law enforcement sequence continues. Notetaking with the antisocial individual can also be used for strategic purposes. It enables the interviewer to take natural pauses (to think or compose questions), to revisit certain issues, and to slow the pace of the interview. You may want to let the interviewee know in a casual way that you will be taking notes just as a routine part of the interview. Many of these individuals have been through the system and are familiar with what normal practice is.

Time Frame

For reasons previously mentioned and that will be discussed in greater detail in the interview section of this chapter, the more time you spend with the antisocial individual, the better. Due to the tendency to want to move too quickly into the interrogation and obtain a confession, many law enforcement officers overlook two important things. First, much of the information gathered during the interview can be valuable during any potential interrogation. Second, the inconsistencies and omissions often found in interviews with antisocial individuals can prove critical during any subsequent legal proceedings, particularly in the absence of a confession.

Review of Records

One area of preparation that is often overlooked is previous interview behavior. Because many antisocial individuals have a history of interactions with law enforcement, you may have the opportunity to review interview reports and speak with detectives, officers, probation and parole officers, or others regarding how the person responded in previous interview settings.

The Interview

Now that you have a good understanding of the behaviors antisocial individuals are likely to engage in during the interview process and the reasons for those behaviors, settled on an effective interview style, and engaged in thorough preparation, it is time for the actual interview. This section cannot be a comprehensive discussion of all you may encounter, but it will address many of the details that increase the likelihood of the interview going well. In this section we use the vignette of Michael presented earlier to emphasize key points made throughout this chapter.

Antisocial individuals have a history of counterproductive interactions with authority figures, beginning with parents, extending to teachers, and on to officials in the criminal justice system. That history has led them to certain expectations about how they will be treated. Their experience may have been with authority figures who were intent on showing their authority in ways that were harsh, condescending, or punitive. Therefore, it is important with antisocial individuals that you establish the right tone from the very beginning to counter those expectations. Before you even begin with an introduction, maintain open body language and seat yourself at the same level as the interviewee. Then you can ease into the interview by introducing yourself in a very casual way, letting the interviewee know who you are and what your position is. For example,

Interviewer: Hi Michael. I'm Dan Martin and I'm with the Sheriff's Department. Before we get started, I just need to get a little background information.

By sitting down, you have placed yourself at his level while the statement itself serves the purpose of initially moving into an area that avoids heightening anxiety, anger, or defensiveness. In addition to being nonthreatening, spending a considerable amount of time gathering biographical data before addressing any substantive issues accomplishes a few important goals. First, it allows you to settle into a conversational interviewing style and become familiar with the interviewee's baseline behavior. The other thing it allows for is the chance to gather potentially valuable information concerning relationships and other areas of his life that may provide some insight as to what is important to him. This becomes important later because antisocial individuals typically evaluate relationships in terms of possible advantages for themselves. Based on prior experiences in this type of setting, or with authority figures in general, it may take time before an interviewee determines how comfortable he is talking to you, or, more importantly, if it is in his best interests to do so.

As the interview progresses, you want to maintain a conversational tone regardless of how the interviewee responds. As you begin to direct the interview toward substantive issues, keep in mind that antisocial individuals tend to be oriented to the present without a great deal of thought or concern for the future. Because of their lack of awareness for future consequences, you want to reinforce the seriousness of the present situation and that it could have serious implications. However, at the same time, you want to counter any potential negative emotions with some sense of hope that they can still help themselves or receive some kind of help. For example,

Interviewer: Look Michael, this is a serious situation. We have to pursue it and we will eventually find out the truth. At this point, we are just trying to gather the facts. We know you were at the bar that night, and I was kind of hoping that you could sit down and tell me what you know.

Michael: Why should I tell you anything?

Interviewer: Well, because it's in your best interest to give me your side of the story. I don't know what happened or who was involved and, for all I know, it could have been completely justified. At this point, I'm really just trying to get a better idea of what took place.

The above language serves the primary goal of the interview, which is to keep the interviewee talking. You began by reinforcing the seriousness of the situation, the fact that the investigation will continue, and that there could be serious implications for someone. Then, telling Michael that it is in his best interest to talk gives the impression that you are looking out for him in some way. However, by not directly accusing him and implying that the actions may have been justified, you are giving him the hope that if he was involved, that he at least may have an avenue to explain or provide information, even if the information is not initially accurate.

Something else to consider is that you may be successful in appealing to something that is advantageous to him at the moment. Antisocial individuals are capable of forming self-serving alliances and of feeling a certain amount of respect for others who can, in a nonjudgmental and face-saving way, address their actions while also showing a willingness to help. You do not want to make promises you cannot fulfill or have no right to offer, but you do want to make them feel assured that, while you have a job to do, you are also there on their behalf. For example,

Interviewer: Look, we don't believe that whoever was involved intended for things to turn out the way they did. It was probably one of those situations of being in the wrong place at the wrong time, and things just got out of hand. We just want to find out the truth about what happened, and then we will do our part to make sure that whoever was involved is treated fairly according to the facts.

Using statements such as the ones above accomplishes several things. First, you address the antisocial tendency to rationalize behaviors and externalize blame to others or the circumstances at the time. Second, the use of the word "we" conveys a sense of alliance between the interviewer and the interviewee, while also reinforcing to the interviewee the power and resources that the interviewer has at his disposal to provide help.

Another important thing to remember is that the ability of the antisocial individual to feel empathy, guilt, or remorse is typically limited; however, the depth of such emotions varies from individual to individual. Yet even when they do experience these emotions, antisocial individuals quickly deny or rationalize their behaviors. So, establishing any real rapport or appealing to their empathy, remorse or guilt is unlikely.

The combination of a sincere, conversational, and nonjudgmental tone; the confidence and competence displayed by the interviewer; and the subtle use of the term "we" is very important. It shows the ASPD individual that the interviewer knows what he or she is doing and is willing to work with the ASPD individual in a mutually beneficial way. Also, when done properly, this method of interviewing tends to convey a sense of respect, which is an effective way of appealing to the ASPD individual's grandiosity and feelings of entitlement. For these individuals, it is not so much about feeding their ego through recognition of their status or accomplishments, but rather about treating them with a measure of respect that appeals to an underlying belief of "I am somebody." In a very ironic way, ASPD individuals perpetually engage in behaviors that, by their very nature, should not earn them any respect, yet they expect a certain amount of respect nonetheless. They want others to appreciate or respect them in terms of their ability to survive and to be thought of as someone to be reckoned with. It is not uncommon, at the end of a successful interview with an ASPD individual, to hear him say something like, "You know something? I like you. You treated me with respect. You treated me like I was somebody." In turn, he seems to develop or have a certain amount of respect for someone who he feels is a worthy adversary but playing the game almost as well as he does. The resulting pseudo-bond that you may experience is really a by-product of this sense of mutual respect that you were able to convey during the interview.

It is always important with these individuals that you maintain a sincere and nonjudgmental tone, no matter what the offense. However, it is especially so at the conclusion or termination of the interview. Regardless of why the interview was terminated, you really want to end the interview on the same casual, friendly level on which it started.

Leave them with the feeling that you were sincere about working together, and that the opportunity will still exist in the future. You do not want to end the interview by aggressing or asserting your power and authority, because it will only reinforce what they already assumed about you, and likely close the door on any future interviews.

Key Points to Remember

Do

- Do be prepared in terms of knowing the case and the history of the interviewee (as much as possible).
- Do maintain a calm, sincere, friendly tone and demeanor.
- Do make sure your body language conveys openness and attentiveness.
- Do understand the importance and potential usefulness of taking your time in the background and biographical information phase.
- Do emphasize the immediacy and seriousness of the situation while also letting the interviewee know that there is hope.
- Do have a number of "face-saving" themes prepared based on the facts of the case.
- Do attempt to develop an atmosphere where the interviewee believes it would be beneficial to form some sort of alliance with the interviewer (rather than developing rapport in the traditional sense of emotional bonding).
- Do treat them with respect.
- Do maintain objectivity. Don't forget that many antisocial people come off as likeable in interpersonal settings and are very good at putting other people at ease. They have learned how to read people well, how to spot vulnerabilities, and how to manipulate those vulnerabilities to their benefit.

Don't

- Don't be confrontational, aggressive, or authoritative.
- Don't get defensive or respond in kind to anger, insults, or other negative behaviors and emotions.

- Don't automatically dismiss the interviewee's ability to feel some level of guilt or remorse, particularly when the act in question was highly impulsive or under the influence of drugs or alcohol.
- Don't be judgmental.
- Don't be punitive.
- Don't make promises that you cannot fulfill.

Reference

American Psychiatric Association. (2000). *Diagnostic and statistical manual of mental disorders (4th ed., text rev.)*. Washington, DC: American Psychiatric Association.

4

THE PSYCHOPATHIC PERSONALITY

The ten o'clock news lead story was an arrest in a series of sexual murders.

"Police announce that they have made an arrest in the series of local murders. Damon Rush was arrested and charged with the sadistic sexual assault and murder of four women. Police describe the victims as being bound, tortured, and viciously sexually assaulted. The investigations revealed that each of the victims had confided in friends that they had met someone who was extremely charming and easy to talk to. Family and friends say it's now clear the victims were being targeted by the killer. Police say very little evidence was left at the crime scenes and that the crimes were premeditated and carried out in a methodical manner.

Rush has been married for seventeen years and has two children. He served four years in the United States Marine Corps and has been employed for the last thirteen years as an engineer with a local chemical plant. Police indicate he has no criminal record. The arrest comes as a shock to friends and neighbors who describe him as a respected member of the community and always ready with a friendly greeting. They said it was hard to believe that the man they know could be responsible for such brutal and sadistic crimes.

As Rush was being led into the courthouse for arraignment, reporters asked if he had anything to say to the victims' families. Rush just smiled and said, 'I'm really more concerned about myself right now.'"

At the age of eight, Tim poured gasoline on a cat, lit it on fire, and watched in pleasure as the tortured animal ran in a confused pattern until it collapsed, writhing in pain. At the age of ten, he was expelled from school for stabbing a classmate in the arm with a pen during an argument. He was first incarcerated in a juvenile facility at the age of fourteen after sexually assaulting a twelve-year-old girl. At nineteen years old, Tim was incarcerated for armed robbery and aggravated assault after holding up a convenience store. During the robbery, he severely injured the clerk by repeatedly striking her in the head with his handgun after she failed to follow his directions. When Tim was twenty-six years old, he had spent nearly a third of his life in juvenile and adult correctional facilities and was in the first year of a six-year sentence for armed robbery. Tim was temporarily housed in a county jail, awaiting arraignment on additional charges. In the middle of the night, he opened the door to his cell (after stuffing toilet paper into the locking mechanism), beat two jailers unconscious with a metal leg from the cot in his cell, and escaped.

Tim and his brother, Shawn, then drove three states away where they stayed with Randy, who had previously been incarcerated with Tim. The three of them spent the next several weeks celebrating by drinking day and night. Running low on money, they decided to rob a liquor store. While Shawn and Randy waited in the car, Tim went into the liquor store. A few minutes later they heard a shot. Tim then walked out of the store, got into the car, and calmly told Shawn, "You better get out of here."

"What the hell happened in there?" Shawn asked nervously.

"I shot some guy," Tim replied in a matter-of-fact tone.

Shawn looked at him incredulously and asked, "What do you mean you shot some guy? What is the matter with you? We're going to have every cop in this city looking for us."

"He asked for it," Tim said with a smile. He then turned to Randy and said, "Shawn's always getting worked up over little things," and then he laughed.

After they returned to the house, they started drinking to celebrate Shawn's birthday. After a couple hours of drinking, Shawn and Randy started arguing. The argument escalated and Shawn started punching Randy. Tim grabbed Shawn and pulled him off Randy. The two of them started fighting and Tim punched Shawn in the jaw, knocking him out. Tim then carried Shawn to the bedroom and threw him on the bed. A short time later, Tim and Randy thought they heard Shawn moving around. Tim said, "Shit, he's still got his gun." He then picked up his gun and walked down the hallway. Randy then heard some yelling and three gunshots. Tim then walked back into the living room and said, "Can you believe it? He made me shoot him on his birthday. Come on, we better do something with him." They buried him in a wooded area behind the house and then went to a local bar. Two weeks later, Tim and Randy robbed a bank and were subsequently arrested after a high-speed chase and shoot-out with law enforcement officers.

Description of the Psychopathic Personality

The two vignettes above describe individuals vastly different from one another in many ways, yet they share one central feature: *psychopathy*. When it comes to defining the psychopathic personality, there seems to be considerable confusion. In fact, psychopathy is often used interchangeably with many other terms, most notably antisocial personality disorder and sociopathy. Psychopathy is not listed as a personality disorder in the current edition of the *Diagnostic and Statistical Manual of Mental Disorders* ([DSM-IV-TR]; American Psychiatric Association, 2000), but it is likely that it will be included in the fifth edition of the DSM, scheduled for publication in 2013 (for updates on DSM-V, see dsm5.org). Even the term "psychopathic personality" is something of an umbrella term, covering several different types of psychopaths. Some psychopaths are criminals, while most are not. Some have little impulse control or self-discipline, while others have high levels of these attributes. Some psychopaths spend their lives in and out of relationships, jobs, and correctional facilities, while others maintain long-term relationships and enjoy successful careers. The reason for these varied life histories is that, although there are several features that define the "core" of the psychopathic personality, the way in which they are expressed depends on a combination of inborn and situational factors.

Within the law enforcement setting, the core features of the psychopathic personality you are likely to encounter revolve around three components: the psychopath's view of himself and others, low levels of fear and anxiety, and emotional deficiencies.

Views of Self and Others

The psychopathic individual's view of himself revolves around a grandiose image, specifically feelings of omnipotence. Omnipotence is not just the feeling of having power and control over others, but *ultimate* power and control over others. This sense of grandiosity leads to the psychopath's primary need to exert power, control, and domination (omnipotent control) to sustain and reinforce that self-image. The psychopathic view of others is twofold. Others are either considered weak and vulnerable, in which case they are easily exploitable; or they are perceived as having the same desire for control, power, and domination as the psychopath, in which case, they have to be defended against or eliminated.

This combination of how psychopaths view themselves and others leads to a view of the world as a place in which each person occupies one of two positions: asserting ultimate power over others versus being dominated and controlled. In essence, the psychopathic world is one of *predator versus prey*—and the psychopath will always attempt to be the predator.

Low Levels of Fear and Anxiety

Fear and anxiety are not the same thing; however, there is an important relationship between the two. Anxiety is the apprehensiveness you experience as you think about potentially risky, dangerous, or embarrassing situations. Fear is the actual perception of potential danger. To clarify this relationship, let's say you have a fear of flying. When you think about getting on a plane, you feel a "knot in your stomach," your heart starts to race, and you begin to sweat. What you are experiencing is anxiety. It is in response to your fear (perception) of something potentially harmful, namely that the plane might crash. Fear can take different forms (e.g., worry, concern, apprehension), and the potential harm can be physical (e.g., injury, death, going to prison) or psychological (e.g., shame, humiliation).

Both anxiety and fear serve an alerting function that helps in the planning and control of behavior that is self-protective and socially appropriate. Psychopaths show little anxiety or fear in those circumstances when it would be normal to do so. As a result, their behavior frequently violates social norms, significantly endangering others in the process.

Emotional Deficiencies

Emotional deficiencies within the psychopathic personality revolve around the inability to develop bonds with others. It is the empathic attachment to others that provides the foundation for emotions such as love, sadness, sympathy, compassion, guilt, and remorse. Ultimately, these emotions lead to the development of loyalty, commitment, and responsibility to and for others, characteristics that are lacking in the predator-versus-prey world of the psychopath.

Associated Features

In essence, the psychopathic need to exert power, control, and domination over others leads to predatory behavior, which can take many forms. Their low levels of fear and anxiety allow them to engage in harmful behavior in calculating ways, without fear of consequences. Their inability to feel empathic emotions and to develop qualities such as loyalty and responsibility allows them to engage in predatory behavior without remorse or guilt. These foundational components lead to numerous associated features, which are discussed below.

For the psychopath, exerting power, control, and domination typically involves conscious manipulative and deceptive behaviors aimed at exploiting others in some way for personal gain. This exploitive behavior can take many forms, ranging from psychological manipulation to brutal physical aggression and from almost imperceptible interactions to overt cruelty. Pathological lying is a prominent feature, both in their exploitation of others and in avoiding the consequences of their actions.

While psychopaths are unable to experience empathic emotions such as the ones described previously, they are able to recognize these emotional displays in others. They also can identify situations when it would be advantageous for them to appear to have such emotions. So, while they have an inability to genuinely experience emotions such as remorse, guilt, or sadness, they do have a remarkable ability to imitate or mimic those emotions behaviorally. Their intense awareness of emotions in others leads not only to the ability to imitate those emotional displays, but also to an incredible adeptness at reading even the most subtle emotional cues. They use these abilities to develop and maintain whatever type of relationship is advantageous to them at the moment. It is only upon close inspection over time that one begins to sense the shallowness of their emotions and the superficial nature of their relationships.

Whether they are subtly manipulating others in relationships or engaging in overt cruelty (psychological or physical), psychopaths lack the ability to feel empathy for their victims. They display a cold, callous indifference to the suffering of others and are unaffected by the distressing emotions their victims may experience or the negative impact of their behaviors. Once they have achieved their goals, no matter how tragic the consequences to their victims, their lack of remorse or guilt allows them to walk away without feeling bad about what they have done. It is the combination of these features that has led to the description of the psychopath as having no conscience or "moral compass."

It is important to remember that having emotional deficiencies means psychopaths do not experience certain emotions in the ways that most people do. It does *not* mean that they are incapable of feeling emotions at all. While they do not experience empathic emotions, they can experience other emotions (e.g., frustration, envy, sadistic pleasure, anger) very intensely. Anger, in particular, is an emotion psychopaths frequently experience. This is usually in response to anything perceived as an assault on their grandiose self-image or the frustration of any goal, urge, or desire. Experiences that are interpreted as positive revolve around reinforcing the psychopathic sense of omnipotence, while experiences that are interpreted as negative revolve around those that contribute to a sense of weakness. Their emotional responses to experiences interpreted as positive do not involve traditional feelings of happiness or joy, but rather a sort of sadistic pleasure, satisfaction, contentment, and even exhilaration. Experiences interpreted as negative do not evoke the typical emotions of fear, sadness, depression, guilt, shame, or remorse, but rather, indifference, frustration, anger, or rage.

The Psychopathic Continuum The best way to begin to conceptualize psychopathy is to look at Figure 4.1. The horizontal continuum represents the ability to bond emotionally with others, including those emotions (e.g., love, sadness, empathy, sympathy, compassion, guilt, and remorse) and qualities (e.g., loyalty, commitment, and responsibility to and for others) associated with genuine attachment. The vertical continuum represents the ability to function well in social and interpersonal settings, the ability to control emotions, level of impulse control, and level of self-discipline.

On the left end (limited ability to feel empathy) of the horizontal continuum, you will see the obliviously narcissistic and antisocial personalities. Each of these personalities has some (albeit limited) ability

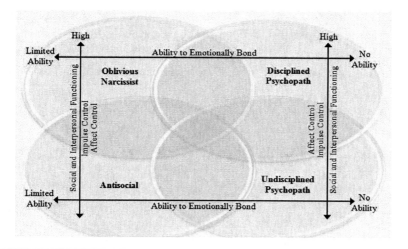

Figure 4.1 The psychopathic continuum.

to emotionally attach with others, feel remorse or guilt, and develop loyalties. Narcissistic and antisocial personalities share a number of features; however, they are differentiated by such things as the ability to function well in social and interpersonal settings, the ability to control emotions, impulse control, and self-discipline. This is represented by the vertical continuum. The oblivious narcissist has a higher level of these social and control characteristics, while the antisocial individual has low levels of each.

On the right side (no ability to feel empathy) of the horizontal continuum are psychopathic personalities. These personalities also exist along the same vertical continuum as the obliviously narcissistic and antisocial personalities. At the top (high end) of the vertical continuum is the psychopath who is disciplined, controlled, and can successfully function within interpersonal, social, and employment settings. In many ways, this disciplined psychopath is an extension of the obliviously narcissistic personality. They share the core feature of a grandiose self-image, leading to the belief that they are superior to others and entitled to special treatment. However, there are also some differentiating features. The oblivious narcissist deals with insult by ignoring or devaluing the insulting person. The disciplined psychopath responds by actively injuring anyone who threatens his grandiosity.

At the bottom (low end) of the vertical continuum is the psychopathic personality who has little to no impulse control or self discipline, is unable to control his emotions (most notably anger), and functions poorly within interpersonal, social, and employment settings. In many ways the undisciplined psychopath is an extension of the antisocial personality in that both frequently end up in the criminal justice system. However, there are important differences, as illustrated by the following examples:

Example 1: Jimmy was incarcerated at a local jail, serving a sentence for an aggravated assault conviction. Another individual, Victor, was placed in the same cellblock as Jimmy while awaiting trial on manslaughter charges after shooting two men. On several occasions, Jimmy overheard Victor bragging to another inmate about killing a woman several years earlier in an area of the city known as Walnut Hills. Victor described how he brutally raped the woman and how he enjoyed looking into her eyes as he continually strangled her to the point where she would almost pass out and then let her breathe, eventually strangling her to death. He also bragged about how the police would never be able to solve the crime. Jimmy subsequently called his girlfriend and his mother and asked them to notify the detective who had arrested Jimmy. The following is from the interview with Jimmy:

Interviewer: Jimmy, you've already been sentenced and, with your history, I doubt I will be able to do anything for you.

Jimmy: I ain't looking for anything. I've got nine months left on my sentence and then I'm out of here.

Interviewer: Then why are you telling me this?

Jimmy: 'Cause it's just wrong.

Interviewer: You know if this goes to trial, you're going to have to testify—

Jimmy: I got no problem with that.

Interviewer: ...and it's going to be difficult to convince a jury that you did this out of the goodness of your heart. You're in jail for shooting somebody, and you've got a long history of burglary, robbery, assault, and drug arrests.

Jimmy: Man, the guy I shot was another drug dealer who pulled a gun on me and was trying to rip me off. I ain't going to deny that I've done a lot of shit and I've hurt some people. But I ain't never hurt anybody that didn't deserve it. I ain't never hurt no kid, I ain't never hurt no woman, and I ain't never done anything like what Victor did. That's just wrong. That could've been my girlfriend or my mother.

Example 2: In the vignette about Tim presented at the beginning of this chapter, we described how Tim shot the manager of a liquor store during a robbery and later shot and killed his own brother after an argument. After reaching a plea agreement, Tim was interviewed about his crimes. The following is from the interview:

Interviewer: Tell me what happened in the liquor store.

Tim: I told the girl behind the counter to give me all of the money from the cash register. While she was doing that, this guy walks up and asked what was going on. I pointed my gun at him and told him if he didn't want to get shot, to shut up and get his ass behind the counter. The girl was crying and fumbling with the cash register. I told her she had about a minute to get the money or I was going to shoot her. Then this guy tells me there was no need to hurt anybody and tells the girl everything was going to be all right. I asked him if he thought he was some kind of a tough guy and he just glared at me, which pissed me off. So I shot him.

Interviewer: Why?

Tim: Just because of the look on his face. It was like he was challenging me...

(Later in the interview)

Interviewer: Let's talk about what happened to your brother.

Tim: Shawn (his brother), Randy, and I went back to the house. We were just sitting around drinking to celebrate Shawn's birthday, when Shawn and Randy got into a fight over something stupid. I tried to pull Shawn off of Randy and we got into it. I ended up knocking Shawn out and then dragged him to the bedroom to sleep it off. A little while later I heard some noise down the hallway and realized I forgot to take Shawn's gun from him. So, I got my gun and started down the hallway. When I got to the bathroom, Shawn was up on the counter and jumped off at me. So, I shot him. As he was laying on the floor, I saw that he was bleeding a lot and in pretty bad shape. So, I shot him two more times.

Interviewer: Didn't it bother you that you killed your own brother?

Tim: No, why should it? I figured it was him or me—and it wasn't going to be me. Anyway, Randy and I buried him out back and went out to have a beer....

Let's compare the two individuals in the above examples. They both display classic features of the antisocial personality described in this book, in particular lengthy criminal histories, little to no impulse control or self-discipline, an inability to control emotional responses (most notably anger), and poor functioning within interpersonal, social, and employment settings. However, there are some distinctive differences between the two.

Jimmy clearly has engaged in numerous instances of criminal behavior, both violent and nonviolent. However, his statement, "I ain't never hurt no kid, I ain't never hurt no woman, and I ain't never done anything like what Victor did. That's just wrong," tells you he has internalized some guidelines to identify behavior that he believes is unacceptable and morally wrong. His statement, "That could've been my girlfriend or my mother," indicates some level of care, concern, and responsibility for others. These statements indicate an ability (albeit limited) to emotionally attach to others, to experience empathic emotions, and to establish a threshold for behavior that he sees as morally unacceptable.

On the other hand, Tim's behaviors show decidedly more psychopathic features. They have a predatory quality and are carried out in a cold, remorseless fashion. Even when his behavior is impulsive, such as when he shot the manager, there is a callous nature to it, and his descriptions in the interview lack any sort of empathic emotion. Anyone who has listened to a psychopath recite the details of his or her violent crime(s) has been struck by the detached, emotionless, matter-of-fact quality to the descriptions. The psychopathic view of the world as one of predator versus prey is summed up in Tim's statement, "I figured it was him or me—and it wasn't going to be me."

In summary, features of the psychopathic personality are described as follows:

- View of self, others, and the world:
  - A grandiose self-image of omnipotence (ultimate power and control)
  - A view of others as:
    - Weak and vulnerable, in which case they are easily exploitable, or
    - Having the same desire for control, power, and domination, in which case they have to be defended against
  - A view of the world in which one occupies a position of either predator or prey

- The need to exert power, control, or domination over others
- Low levels of fear and anxiety:
  - A limited ability to experience fear and anxiety in situations that would evoke those emotions for most people
  - A limited ability to anticipate negative consequences
  - A limited ability to control behavior as a result of negative consequences
- Emotional deficiencies:
  - A limited ability to experience empathic emotions (e.g., love, sadness, empathy, sympathy, compassion, guilt, or remorse)
  - A limited ability to develop related empathic qualities (e.g., loyalty, commitment, responsibility to and for others)
- Associated features:
  - A remarkable ability to imitate or mimic empathic emotions
  - An adeptness at reading subtle emotional cues in others
  - A view of empathic emotions in others as weaknesses to be exploited
  - Ability to experience other emotions (e.g., frustration, envy, sadistic pleasure, anger) intensely
  - Superficial relationships
  - Extremely uninhibited behavior in their interactions with others
  - Exploitation of others
  - Manipulative and deceptive behaviors
  - Pathological lying
  - Inability to feel empathy (cold, callous indifference to the suffering of others)
  - Lack of remorse or guilt
  - Appearance of having no conscience or "moral compass."
- Disciplined versus undisciplined:
  - In addition, psychopathic personalities exist on a continuum regarding their ability to function well in social and interpersonal settings, to control emotions, to control impulses, and to maintain self-discipline.

Assessing the Psychopathic Personality

This section is not designed to exhaust all sources of information an investigator may utilize to conduct an indirect assessment of a potential interviewee. Rather, it is designed to present a number of questions that address the core features of psychopathy discussed throughout this chapter and to offer some suggestions regarding sources of information typically most useful in answering those questions. Remember that psychopathic features exist on a continuum. These questions are *not* for the purpose of diagnosing the interviewee with a personality disorder, but rather for determining the presence and strength of psychopathic features of his or her personality. For the purposes of clarity, this section is written for the assessment of a male interviewee.

As previously described, psychopathic individuals have much in common with individuals with narcissistic and antisocial personalities. More often than not, the characteristics of the psychopath overlap with at least one of these other personalities. The questions we are suggesting will help in identifying the psychopathic aspects in what is often a complex picture.

In assessing psychopathy, we have organized our questions into three subsections. The first involves characteristics that go toward the core of psychopathy. These questions address the interrelated components of psychopathy: view of self and others, low level of fear and anxiety, and emotional deficiencies. The second subsection includes questions regarding the psychopathic individual on the disciplined end of the continuum. The final subsection includes questions regarding the psychopathic personality on the undisciplined end of the continuum.

Core Questions

- Is he unable to develop close emotional bonds with others? Do his relationships seem to be superficial or shallow in nature? Do his friendships with others lack those things that you typically find in close relationships (e.g., concern, care, loyalty, commitment)? In relationships, would others say he is only concerned with himself?

- Does he typically appear unaffected by stressful situations that would ordinarily upset most people? Does he seem to lack anxiety? Does he show little to no nervousness when it would be typical to do so?
- Does he show little anxiety when interacting with other people? Is he comfortable in interpersonal settings? In other words, does it seem like he does not worry about embarrassing himself around others or making a social blunder?
- Would people say that he acts without fear of or concern for the consequences of his behavior?
- Does he appear unaffected by situations when others would typically show emotions such as sadness or sympathy? Does it seem like he never really feels bad, guilty, or experiences any remorse, even when he wrongs someone?
- Does he demonstrate an attitude of indifference or a cold, callous demeanor?
- Would people say he is indifferent to the suffering of others?
- Does he think he is superior to others? Does he treat others as inferior, in a way that is condescending or dismissive?
- Does he seem to need to exert control over or dominate others? Does he feel the need to show others who is boss?
- Does he show intense feelings of anger or frustration at times, particularly when his image is threatened or when his goals are obstructed?
- Does he react vindictively when he feels someone has gotten the better of him?
- Does he refuse to accept blame or take responsibility for his actions when he should?
- Would people say he views situations or evaluates others in terms of how they can be used to serve his needs? Does he use others for his own benefit? Does he frequently take advantage of others?
- Is he manipulative in his dealings with others? Is he straightforward with others, or do others think he has ulterior motives?
- Does he use charm as a means to manipulate others?
- Does he like to "toy" with others or show that he can outsmart other people?

- Does he frequently lie?
- Would people describe him as lacking a conscience or as having no morals?

Answers to the above questions should help give you some indication of whether or not you are dealing with a psychopathic personality. Gathering information to answer the questions in the following two subsections will help you determine where that psychopathic personality falls on the continuum ranging from disciplined to undisciplined.

The Disciplined Psychopath

In addition to the core questions addressed above, answering yes to some of the following questions may indicate a psychopathic personality on the disciplined end of the spectrum.

- Does he have adequate self-discipline? In other words, can he carry through on plans he has made?
- Has he achieved some level of education?
- Has he managed to establish some level of success or consistency in his employment?
- Does he function fairly well in social, interpersonal, and employment settings?
- Has he been able to maintain some long-term relationships (although they may not be emotionally close relationships)?

The Undisciplined Psychopath

In addition to the core questions, answering yes to some of the following questions may indicate a psychopathic personality on the undisciplined end of the spectrum.

- Does he have little or no impulse control? In other words, does he act without thinking?
- Would people say he has difficulty controlling his emotions, particularly anger?
- Does he lack self-discipline?

- Does he have a history of sporadic employment and/or short-term relationships?
- Does he have a criminal record or a history of problems with authority?
- Would he be described as irresponsible, unreliable, and undependable?

Preparation Issues

Preparation is a critical aspect of any interview. This section is intended to provide you with an understanding of those issues that are important considerations as you prepare to interview the psychopathic individual.

Understanding Your Reactions to the Individual

One of the central features of psychopathic personalities is the need to exert control, power, and domination over others, and this need can play out in a variety of ways. At any moment, psychopaths can either display a chameleon-like ability to take on any persona they deem necessary, or they can reveal the cold, dominating, nonempathic nature that is their true character. Whatever behavior they engage in, it is ultimately done to achieve the goal that is important to them at the moment. Being prepared for these different types of behavior and understanding your instinctive reactions will allow you to recognize them and avoid responding in ways that are counterproductive. The following are some of the most common behaviors you are likely to encounter and the ways in which you are likely to respond:

- *Attacking and/or hostile behavior:* Many psychopaths will attempt to exert direct control over the interview through behavior that is condescending, sarcastic, dismissive, or in some way designed to make the interviewer feel inferior. They may try in some way to diminish your intellect, investigative abilities, authority, or credibility. Their attempts to provoke these responses are twofold. First, they take particular delight in any opportunity to shame or humiliate you. Second, provoking these responses gives them a sense of control. The natural tendency for most people is to experience feelings of annoyance, irritation, frustration, anger, or defensiveness in the face of such behavior.

- *Friendly and charming behavior:* Psychopaths are very much at ease in their interactions with others, are adept at reading emotional cues, and have a remarkable ability to mimic whatever empathic emotion is necessary to achieve their goal. Not all psychopaths are charming, but those who are can use these abilities to manipulate even the most experienced interviewer (most of whom have undoubtedly bought into a convincing "emotional performance" by a psychopath at one point or another). Their skills have been refined through a lifetime of attempting to manipulate every person and situation they have encountered and should never be underestimated. A common reaction that interviewers have when faced with this behavior are thoughts and feelings such as, "He is not really that bad a guy," "Maybe he didn't really mean to do it," "I really want to help him," or "Maybe he didn't do it." It is easy to believe you are establishing a real bond or rapport when psychopaths are being friendly and charming, or to naturally feel empathy and sympathy when they are acting remorseful. Just remember, you are feeling what they want you to feel. When you begin to experience these responses, evaluate your reaction carefully in relation to the factual details of the case.

- *Sexually manipulative behavior:* While this type of behavior can be seen with either gender, it is particularly prevalent among female psychopaths with male interviewers. This behavior can range from subtle gestures and remarks to blatant sexual advances. Most of us are susceptible, to some degree, to appeals to our egos. Psychopaths who are sexually manipulative are very good at quickly spotting those individuals who might be vulnerable to this type of behavior and exploiting it to their benefit. The instinctive reaction when faced with this behavior is similar to that described above: to want to think well of, help, or protect the interviewee. Again, when you begin to experience these responses, evaluate your reaction carefully in relation to the factual details of the case and the individual's history.

- *"Game" behavior:* Remember that the psychopathic view of the world is one of predator versus prey, and much of their behavior is organized around the principle of "getting over on people." In many ways, they view life as sort of a "chess game," and they all believe they are "chess masters." Within the interview setting, psychopaths who engage in this type of behavior enjoy being the focus of attention, "outsmarting" the interviewer, or "getting to" the interviewer. They exhibit a condescending air of amusement as they attempt to disrupt and direct the interview through a variety of means, such as avoiding direct answers to questions, giving hypothetical answers, answering questions with questions, making demands, invading the interviewer's personal space, provoking emotional responses, and talking at length about themselves or irrelevant matters. This type of behavior provokes frustration and overwhelming urges to let the interviewee know who is in charge.

While these are common behaviors of psychopaths during interviews, this summary certainly does not encompass all possibilities. As discussed, your instinctive responses can vary, depending on the type of behavior you are faced with, and it is important to prepare yourself for any eventuality.

Who Should Conduct the Interview

Understanding the psychopathic personality and what you are likely to encounter within the interview setting is critical in conducting an effective interview. It is equally critical that you possess the right combination of personality traits or features, given the information discussed to this point, in order to have the best chance of a successful outcome.

Psychopathic personalities have a primary need to exert control, power, and domination over others, and the interview setting is no different. Because of this need and the ways in which they attempt to achieve it, there are several important qualities the interviewer must possess: the ability to keep his or her ego in check; the ability to avoid showing, verbally or nonverbally, any emotions he or she may experience during the interview; and the ability to accurately assess and recall both the facts of the case and the information provided by the interviewee.

First and foremost, if you are faced with behavior that is arrogant, condescending, sarcastic, dismissive, or in some other way designed to make you feel inferior, you must be able to tolerate it comfortably. Keeping your ego in check is much more than resisting the urge to show you are in control, smarter, or more competent. It is about feeling comfortable in giving up *perceived* control of the environment, allowing the psychopath to feel that he is running the show.

The interview of the psychopath is not the place for an interviewer who cannot conceal his or her emotions. In other words, you need to be able to maintain the ultimate "poker face." Reading emotional cues is one of the primary ways in which psychopaths control and manipulate others. Not only do they look for emotional signals, but they also try to provoke them. Showing negative emotions such as anger, defensiveness, or frustration can interfere with your ability to conduct an effective interview by clouding your judgment. In addition, psychopaths will view the display of such emotions as a loss of control on your part and will seize the opportunity to make you lose focus, reveal information you might not want to, provoke confrontation, or simply to amuse themselves. Showing positive emotions, such as satisfaction or pleasure when you feel the interview is going your way, will be viewed by psychopaths as a change in the power differential, suggesting you have gained the upper hand. This will cause them to feel threatened, in which case they will launch into a predatory attack in an attempt to regain control. Therefore it is essential that the interviewer possess the ability to remain calm and keep his or her emotions in check, resisting the urge to react both verbally and nonverbally.

Perhaps the greatest advantage you have in an interview with a psychopath is familiarity with the facts and circumstances of the case. The ability not only to know your case in precise detail but also to recall those details accurately at any time during the interview is crucial. Equally important is the related ability to assess and recall information provided by the interviewee. When combined, these abilities will allow you to detect even the slightest inaccuracies, inconsistencies, omissions, or lies on the part of the interviewee. It will also keep the psychopath from exploiting any lack of knowledge or preparedness on your part. Remember that psychopaths are adept at spotting and exploiting vulnerability or weakness, however slight.

With psychopathic personalities, the gender and age of the interviewer can become important, depending upon the facts and circumstances of the case and the specific interviewee. For example, employing a male interviewer with a sexually manipulative female psychopath or a female interviewer with a friendly and charming male psychopath can be advantageous, giving the interviewee the sense of control he or she needs. In most instances, however, gender and age make little difference. The key is understanding the ways in which the interviewee is likely to exert control, the responses he or she is seeking, suppressing those instinctive responses that would be counterproductive, and, instead, responding in those ways most likely to give the interviewee a sense of control.

As always, a thoughtful, honest self-evaluation on the part of the interviewer is crucial. Typically, the law enforcement officer who is assigned the case conducts the interview. If, however, it is determined that someone else would be better suited, that determination should take precedence in order to increase the likelihood of the interview's success.

Number of Interviewers

We would suggest one interviewer. The psychopathic interviewee will be concerned primarily with controlling and manipulating the interview. His immediate goal may be to gain information, provoke emotions, create discomfort, disrupt the flow of the interview, or simply to amuse himself. However, underneath it all is the need to exert control. The more interviewers present, the greater the ability for psychopathic individuals to gain control by playing one interviewer against the other.

Physical Space/Environment/Interpersonal Space

Given the psychopathic individual's low level of general anxiety, grandiose self-image, and confidence in his or her abilities, the location of the interview typically has little impact on the outcome. We recommend keeping a professional distance with regard to interpersonal space.

Nonverbal Behavior

With psychopathic individuals, you want to be careful about the emotions you convey through eye contact, facial expressions, and body language. They typically are skilled at catching even the most subtle nuances in the expressions and behavior of others and exploiting them for their own advantage. Your eye contact and nonverbal behavior should convey sincerity, a confident strength without being threatening, firmness without being controlling, and the respect the psychopathic individual believes he or she deserves. Make sure to avoid expressions and body language that are empathic in nature (e.g., conveying sadness, sympathy, comfort). Again, psychopaths are unaffected by empathic expressions or gestures but they will look for them as weaknesses to exploit. Prolonged eye contact is acceptable as long as it is in the context of the conversation; however, you want to avoid prolonged eye contact during extended silences. This is particularly true if there is any sense of hostility or uncooperativeness. Remember, the psychopathic world is one of predator versus prey. You will not win any staring contests, nor will they be productive. Prolonged eye contact in that context will only be interpreted as a challenge or a threat.

Questions

Typically, it is best to use open-ended questions while maintaining an overall structure to the interview and keeping careful track of the details. The lack of anxiety when interacting with others and a grandiose sense of superiority combine to fuel the psychopath's unwavering belief that he can talk his way out of any situation. Therefore, you want to ask open-ended questions that give the opportunity for lengthier responses, thereby increasing the chances of capturing inconsistencies, contradictions, omissions, and lies.

Recording the Interview (Notetaking, Audio/Visual Recording)

As with oblivious narcissists and antisocial personalities, notetaking can offer a subtle means of staying in control of the interview. It allows you to maintain structure, remain methodical and detail oriented, and regulate the pace of the interview. It also allows the interviewer to take natural pauses (to think or compose questions) and to revisit certain issues under the guise of being able to clarify the notes. Audio and video recording is recommended. It is not uncommon for psychopaths to talk in as much detail as the interviewer elicits. It is also not uncommon for them to continually contradict themselves or completely change explanations when pressed to provide details. Audio and video recordings are the best means to capture the quantity and accuracy of the information provided. They should be addressed as a matter of policy in order to ensure the accuracy of the interview for the protection of the interviewee. Regardless of whether you use audio or video recording, notetaking is still recommended for the above stated reasons.

Time Frame

Be prepared for a lengthy interview with psychopathic individuals. As previously stated, it is common for them to talk for as long as the interviewer is willing. In addition, it is also common for them to make every effort to manipulate and control the interview in a variety of ways, all of which tend to redirect the interview and cause the interviewer to spend time dealing with irrelevant information and issues.

The Interview

Now that you have a good understanding of the behaviors psychopathic individuals are likely to engage in during the interview process and the reasons for those behaviors, settled on an effective interview style, and thoroughly reviewed the details of the case, it is time for the actual interview. This section cannot be a comprehensive discussion of all you may encounter, but it will address many of the details that increase the likelihood of the interview going well.

Probably more than with any other personality, navigating through an interview with a psychopathic individual presents an unending challenge. While the core features of this personality remain consistent, the ways in which they manifest can change from individual to individual and from minute to minute. Within the subsection entitled, "Understanding Your Reactions to the Individual," we described four common types of psychopathic behavior in the interview setting: attacking and hostile behavior, friendly and charming behavior, sexually manipulative behavior, and "game" behavior. While each of these is different in important respects, they share the core motivation of controlling the interview. Think of it in this way: *Psychopathic individuals typically possess a supreme confidence in their ability to exert control in any situation. However, the manner in which they choose to do so depends on additional traits and qualities they may or may not possess and the situation in which they are trying to exert control.* In this section we discuss each of these behaviors within the interview setting.

Information from interviews and other sources of information prior to the interview are crucial to identifying the nature of the psychopathic personality with which you are dealing. The initial stages of the interview itself provide you with an additional opportunity to get an indication of the type of behavior you will face. Many psychopathic individuals will initially talk to you because of their grandiose self-image, belief in their own abilities, and low anxiety in interpersonal settings. For this reason, it is recommended that you take your time gathering biographical and background information. During this time, you can gauge such things as the level of apparent cooperativeness, level and manner of friendliness (both verbal and nonverbal behavior), and directness of responses. This will allow you to determine the predominant way in which a given interviewee might attempt to exert control over the interview and also the ways in which you need to respond to increase your chances of the interview continuing.

Attacking and/or Hostile Behavior

Psychopathic individuals who engage in attacking and hostile behavior present perhaps the greatest challenge in regard to gathering information. While they may not initially terminate the interview, they are typically far from cooperative. Much like the oblivious narcissist, the psychopath continually has to be in the "one-up" position, exerting superiority, dominance, and control. The difference between the two is that the oblivious narcissist needs to control the environment for threats against self-esteem while, for the psychopath, the need for control is more representative of that pervasive predator-versus-prey worldview.

This aggressiveness can take many forms, such as demeaning your investigative abilities, authority, credibility, intellect, or other personal attributes; direct (or prolonged) eye contact and invading personal space; focusing on one interviewer and completely ignoring the other; derisively comparing and contrasting the qualities of the interviewers; and making demands (e.g., requesting to see evidence, interview notes, or case material; or requesting different interviewers).

We cannot overemphasize the importance of understanding that the primary goal of psychopathic personalities is to control the interview. The important thing to remember is that you do not want to battle with them for control of the interview or you will spend the entire interview battling. Again, we want to stress that there is a difference between *not asserting control* of the interview and *giving up control* of the interview. We are not suggesting that you give up actual control of the interview, only that you allow the interviewee's perception of being in control to go unchallenged. In this way, his sense of comfort and superiority remains intact.

The primary way in which you allow the perception of control is through the manner in which you respond to aggressiveness. It is crucial that your responses not reflect any feelings of anger, annoyance, irritation, or defensiveness, or any attempt to show the interviewee that you are the one who is in charge. Instead, try to respond in ways that subtly reinforce the interviewee's sense of control. Consider the following example:

Scenario: Robert Kendrick was suspected of killing his wife. He had reported her missing and filed a report with the police department. The investigation leading up to the interview disclosed that Kendrick was extremely controlling of his wife, who was fifteen years younger than he was. She had started seeing another man and had confided in others that she wanted to leave Robert but was afraid of what he would do. Robert apparently learned of her affair three days before he reported her missing. He provided an initial statement that he suspected she might have run off with someone, but he had been generally uncooperative in the investigation.

Interviewee: I don't know why you want to talk to me; I already told the police everything I know when I filed the report. Instead of wasting my time and yours, why don't you guys do your jobs and find out what happened to my wife?

Interviewer: I know your time is valuable, Mr. Kendrick, and I'm sorry to be taking so long with you. I am just trying to get all of the information I can at this point. You know your wife better than anyone and you are obviously a bright man, so I was hoping you might be able to give me some insight into your wife's daily routine, habits, friends, or anything else that you think might be helpful in finding her. Can you tell me how she typically spends her days?

Responding in kind to derogatory statements will only result in continued aggressive behavior and could ultimately shut down the interview. Instead, through the use of self-effacing language and statements or questions that appeal to the interviewee's ego (e.g., appeals to his importance, intelligence, competence, etc.), the perception is that he is in a position of power and control. In the above example, you address the interviewee by his last name, conveying respect, and appeal to both his importance and his intelligence. You further provide a sense of control by suggesting that you need help in the investigation. You minimize the issue itself by not addressing his wife by name, using present tense and non-inflammatory language, and by referencing his initial statement. You then conclude with a general, open-ended question that is nonthreatening in nature. All of this enhances the possibility of decreasing the interviewee's hostile behavior and prolonging the interview.

Friendly and Charming Behavior

Psychopathic individuals who have the ability to exhibit convincingly friendly and charming behaviors offer perhaps the easiest interviews with regard to gathering information. They tend to be extroverted individuals with refined interpersonal skills (even youthful psychopathic offenders can be surprisingly articulate) and an unwavering confidence in their ability to explain away any situation or talk themselves out of any predicament. As a result, they will often talk at length within the interview setting because that is the way in which they feel they can best control the situation.

Not all psychopaths are charming and likeable, but those who are demonstrate an ease in interacting with others, an adeptness at reading emotional cues, and a remarkable ability to imitate empathic emotions to manipulate even the most experienced interviewer. While we refer to these individuals as friendly and charming, keep in mind that the emotions they mimic can take other forms, such as remorse or sadness.

There is a natural and instinctive tendency not only to let down your guard around individuals who exhibit this type of behavior, but also to attribute positive qualities such as honesty and sincerity without any real evidence. It is not just their disarming behavior, but also their apparent cooperativeness and willingness to answer questions that can draw you in and cause you to lose track of what questions you need to ask and the overall objective of the interview.

With these individuals it is not so much about countering behaviors as it is about their perception that they have drawn you in. Convey a friendly demeanor and avoid aggressive, confrontational, and accusatory behavior. Use open-ended questions to elicit narrative responses and concentrate on drawing out the details. Consider the following example:

Scenario: Gary was suspected of killing his wife, Kelly, and then staging her death as a suicide. The investigation leading up to the interview indicated that Gary was physically and psychologically abusive in the relationship and that his wife had made arrangements to leave him on the day of her death.

Interviewer: Were you having any problems in your marriage?

Interviewee: Nothing more than what all couples go through. But we worked them out and were closer than ever. We loved each

other very much. This is really a horrible thing that happened. I still can't believe it (shaking his head with a look
of dismay).

Interviewer: It sounds as if you had a good marriage, Gary. Tell me
about the kinds of things you did with each other.

Rather than focusing on information that the interviewee was abusive and that his wife was preparing to leave him, you adopt an interested demeanor and begin to elicit details of the relationship. This
accomplishes several things. First, the reinforcement of his description of a good marriage and the use of his first name in your response
suggest that you have been drawn into a supportive, friendly relationship, thus allowing the interviewee to have a sense of control. Second,
you begin to direct the interview toward having him describe in detail
his relationship with his wife. By doing so, you increase your chances
of obtaining information that differs from evidence you already have
and that you can use later in the interview.

Sexually Manipulative Behavior

Psychopathic individuals who engage in sexually manipulative behavior rely on many of the same abilities as those who engage in friendly
and charming behaviors; however, they also perceive themselves as
possessing a high level of sexual desirability. Very early in the interview process, you can typically observe the differences in the way they
interact with men versus women. With interviewers of the same gender as themselves, their behavior can often become dismissive, condescending, or outright hostile and attacking. If both male and female
interviewers are present, it is not uncommon for these individuals to
interact immediately and exclusively with the interviewer of the opposite sex. While this type of behavior can be seen with either gender, it
is particularly prevalent among female psychopaths. They often possess the physical attributes necessary for this to be an effective strategy
and typically have a history of using their sexuality to control and
manipulate others. Within the interview setting, this behavior can
range from subtle gestures and remarks to blatant sexual advances.
For example,

Interviewee: If I have to be in this room all day, at least it's nice to be interviewed by a good-looking man...

Interviewer: Thanks *(smile)*. Before we get started, I'd like to just take a few minutes and get some background information from you.

—or—

Interviewee: (leaning forward and touching the interviewer's hand) You know, this could be much more fun if we talked somewhere else...maybe over a drink...

Interviewer: (smiling while reaching for a file, a pen, or some other object that provides the opportunity to tactfully pull his hand away) I'm sure it would, but policy says we need to do this here. Now, can you tell me...?

The instinctive reactions to this type of behavior can range from discomfort to feeling flattered and to wanting to think well of the interviewee. The challenging aspect with the sexually manipulative psychopath is to find a way in which to acknowledge the behavior without crossing professional boundaries or being overtly dismissive or critical. It is never acceptable to engage in flirtatious or other unprofessional behavior. At the same time, dismissive or critical responses tend to adversely affect the interview. Therefore, as demonstrated in the above examples, you want to try to respond in ways that achieve both objectives and keep the interview on track.

Female psychopaths may also engage in a common variation of sexually manipulative behavior that presents as the proverbial "damsel in distress." This behavior is designed specifically to appeal to their perception of an instinctual sense of "chivalry" in men, that is a tendency to want to protect and help women who appear vulnerable and distressed. Consider the following example:

Scenario: Sandra was suspected of killing her two-year-old son, Matthew, and staging an abduction. She claimed he had been taken while she left him unattended in a shopping cart at a grocery store on Sunday evening. Early investigation disclosed she had gone through a bitter divorce and her ex-husband had filed for full custody of their son based on evidence she had been physically abusive to the child.

She told her husband on Friday night, after a heated argument, that she would make sure he never got custody of their son. Matthew had not been seen after Friday night.

Interviewee: You have to help me find my son. I don't know what else to do at this point (*sobbing and looking pleadingly at the interviewer*). Please, please help me.

Interviewer: I know this is very difficult for you and I am going to do everything I can to help you find Matthew. We need to begin by going over everything you did and everywhere you went, starting Friday morning and leading up to the time he was taken.

Interviewee: I don't understand how that has anything to do with what happened to my son.

Interviewer: It is very possible that whoever took Matthew may have been following you to study your routine, habits, or just waiting for the right moment when you were most vulnerable. So let's start from the time you got up on Friday morning. What did you do, and where did you go?

Rather than confronting Sandra with information indicating she may have been responsible for what happened to her son, the use of empathic language, demeanor, and tone all exemplify the response that her behavior was intended to elicit, thus reinforcing her sense of control. Through your explanation of what you want to talk about, you reference her account of what took place. By asking to begin before the critical time frame of Friday night through Sunday evening, you further reinforce a nonthreatening tone to the interview. All of this serves to enhance your chances of achieving your primary objective, which is to elicit as much detail as possible.

"Game" Behavior

"Game" behavior is another tactic used by psychopaths to gain control over their "opponent." Remember that the psychopathic view of the world is one of predator versus prey, and much of their behavior is organized around the principle of "getting over on people." They view life as sort of a "chess game" and may try to outsmart you. When psychopaths exhibit this type of behavior, it is critical that you emerge as a worthy opponent. Because of this predator-versus-prey view of the world, these individuals look at the interview process as a challenge. It will sometimes provide motivation for them to talk, in the sense that it is one more arena in which they want to come out victorious. Also, many of them like the social aspects of the interview process and the stimulation that it brings, particularly for those who have been incarcerated for a while. You must convey yourself as experienced, competent, and bright without being overly so. In other words, you do not want to come off in such a way that gives them the feeling that you think less of them. Essentially, you want to be equal opponents with neither person in a one-down position. In this way, you have a better chance of developing that mutual respect for one another that is necessary to maintain subtle control throughout the interview.

Psychopaths who utilize "game" behavior may also exhibit a condescending air of amusement as they attempt to disrupt and direct the interview through a variety of means (e.g., avoiding direct answers to questions, giving "hypothetical" answers, answering questions with questions, making demands, provoking emotional responses, or talking at length about irrelevant matters). Allow them to talk, but then tactfully refocus to get them back on track.

Another strategy in dealing with "game" behavior is to suggest that you could learn from the interviewee, or that he or she might be able to provide some unique insight. This is typically most useful in those instances in which the interviewee questions the logic or legitimacy of a particular theory, assertion, or investigative activity or direction. This strategy can be effective from several perspectives. First, you essentially give the interviewee an open forum with the opportunity to talk. Once he or she is talking, you can direct the interview in the direction you need to go. Second, while the interviewee is talking in hypothetical terms, the responses may provide insight into underlying motivations and details of the incident itself.

General Considerations

Remember that psychopaths have emotional deficiencies that prevent them from developing close emotional bonds or feeling associated emotions such as empathy, guilt, and remorse. Because of their inability to attach, you will never really be able to establish any sort of rapport with psychopathic individuals. However, because of their extraordinary ability to manipulate others, you may be lured into believing you have established a bond. Never underestimate their ability to manipulate you within an interview setting. Even the most experienced interviewer has fallen prey to a psychopathic "performance" at one point or another. Additionally, attempts to appeal to empathic emotions such as guilt or remorse for the victim, the victim's family, or others will likely be ineffective.

In addition, their emotional deficiencies may lead them to discuss their actions in a calm, nonempathic, and matter-of-fact manner. Listening to psychopaths rationalize and describe their behavior in this way can sometimes upset even the most experienced law enforcement professionals. While this is behavior typically encountered during confessions to crimes, it may also occur during the interview setting. Consider the following example:

Scenario: Chris was suspected of abducting a thirteen-year-old girl from a local mall, sexually assaulting her, and then murdering her.

Interviewee: I saw a picture of her in the paper. I don't know nothing about it, but my guess is she probably brought it on herself.

Interviewer: Why do you say that?

Interviewee: C'mon, you know what I mean. Just at that age where they ain't had it yet, but you and I both know they want it. My guess is she came on to him and got what she was asking for, and probably enjoyed it too *(suspect smiles).*

While in many cases their callous behavior is simply the result of an inability to feel empathy or remorse, in other cases, such as the one above, psychopaths take a sadistic pleasure in attempts to provoke distressing emotions such as horror, shock, disgust, disbelief, and anger. Eliciting these emotions is a tactic used to gain some sense of control or power over the interviewer. It is important that you maintain composure and resist the urge to react to these emotions. By revealing your feelings, you run the risk of giving the interviewee the impression that they have gained some sense of power and control over you.

As previously stated, the greatest advantage you possess when interviewing psychopathic individuals is familiarity with the facts and circumstances of your case. With the psychopath, you want to continually elicit as much detail as possible. When pressed for details, psychopaths tend to omit information that they believe is incriminating, admit facts they believe are harmless or that they cannot deny, and outright lie when necessary. The ability to know your case in precise detail will allow you to detect even the slightest inaccuracies, inconsistencies, omissions, or lies. With psychopathic individuals, you always want to be cautious regarding the manner in which you approach inaccuracies, inconsistencies, or lies. Direct and aggressive challenges or confrontation can quickly provoke a hostile response or shut down the interview. For this reason, you need to challenge in more subtle ways and with a tone and demeanor that is nonthreatening. Interestingly, when challenged in this manner, many psychopaths simply change their account in whatever way is necessary to explain the inconsistency.

Because of their low level of anxiety, psychopathic individuals tend not to be susceptible to bluffs, empty threats, or efforts to intimidate them. Attempts to do so will most likely provoke hostile responses or shut down the interview. In addition, you need to remember that these individuals have accumulated a lifetime of experience in reading or manipulating others. As a result, they are adept at seeing through strategies that are obvious or employed in an unconvincing manner.

In conclusion, given the many different presentations of the psychopathic personality, preparing for this interview is probably more difficult than for any other personality discussed in this book. As opposed to going into the interview with a more concrete understanding of what to expect (as well as a more definite approach prepared), with the psychopath, your approach is more reactive, and may change from one moment to the next. Remember that whatever the presentation, if it is not working or if they are being challenged, they are likely to revert to an attacking or hostile style. Typically, psychopathic individuals do not confess unless it is advantageous to them in some way (e.g., reduced punishment through cooperation when evidence in the case is overwhelming, need for recognition or admiration). Therefore, your primary goals with any psychopathic interviewee are to keep them talking and to gather as much detail as possible. The more detailed the interview, the greater the number of inconsistencies, lies, and omissions you are likely to capture and the greater your chances are of an ultimately successful outcome.

Key Points to Remember

Do

- Do allow the perception that the individual is in control.
- Do maintain control of your emotions (both positive and negative) and your nonverbal behavior.
- Do stay focused against attempts to lead you off track.
- Do know all the facts of the case, inside and out.
- Do resist the urge to exert control or act dismissively.
- Do conduct yourself with professionalism.
- Do use open-ended questions.
- Do maintain objectivity.
- Do treat the person with respect.

Don't

- Don't become defensive.
- Don't attempt to use empathy.
- Don't be influenced by seemingly convincing emotional displays.
- Don't attempt to establish rapport.
- Don't be confrontational.

Reference

American Psychiatric Association. (2000). *Diagnostic and statistical manual of mental disorders (4th ed., text rev.)*. Washington, DC: American Psychiatric Association.

5

THE BORDERLINE PERSONALITY

Bob's cell phone rang. He looked at the number and began to panic. He did not want to answer but knew he must. He muttered to himself, "It's her...again." He picked up the phone, "Bob, I love you, why can't you understand it? We had an amazing night together." Bob sighed heavily and said, "Marilyn, it was only one night. How can you say that you love me?" Marilyn screamed into the phone, "What do you mean it was only one night? I don't just sleep with anyone. Do you think I'm a whore? You can't ignore what we have between us. What we have is special. I need to talk with you in person. Meet me tonight." Bob hesitantly said, "I can't tonight." Marilyn threatened, "If you don't meet me tonight, I'll tell your girlfriend," and hung up. Then she immediately called back, apologizing, "This is upsetting me so much. I don't mean to hurt you. Please, you've got to meet with me, I need to talk with you in person." Bob said, "Look, Marilyn, I have to get back to work. I'll have to call you back."

Bob hung up the phone and walked down the hall to the office of his coworker and best friend, Bill. Panicked, he said, "Look, I need to talk to you about something." Bill looked up from his computer and saw that Bob looked rather shaken. Bob went on to tell him about Marilyn, stating, "I met this girl in a bar three weeks ago. I had had too much to drink and ended up going home with her. I realized it was a mistake afterward and I've tried everything I can to tactfully get away from her but she won't leave me alone. It's like she's crazy. She calls me twenty times a day, leaving me messages. In one message she's calmly telling me how much she loves me and in the next one she's screaming at me and making threats. It's getting worse. She's left notes and roses and things on my car. It's like she's stalking me. I go to the gym and she's there … the coffee shop, she's there. And no matter what I do, nothing works. I don't know what to do at this point. She knows where I live. She's actually threatened to kill herself. She's threatened to tell my girlfriend. I'm scared to death. She's just so unstable that I'm afraid that she might hurt herself or my girlfriend or me. I think she could actually do it. What do I do?"

Bill replied, "Bob, she is stalking you. What you need to do is go to the police."

"But," Bob said, "I don't want my girlfriend to find out." Bill responded, "Bob, you've got bigger problems than that. She's clearly exhibiting erratic behavior. What if she hurts you or your girlfriend? Like I said, you need to go to the police."

After talking with Bill, Bob decided to meet with Marilyn, one more time, in an effort to convince her that they had no future together and that there was nothing between them. During the conversation, Marilyn started crying hysterically, begging him not to end their "relationship." He attempted to console her and apologized for everything, but made it clear that it was over and not to contact him anymore. As he walked out to his car, she followed, alternating between screaming threats against him and yelling, "That bitch is coming between us," and pleading with him to stay with her. Not knowing what else to do, Bob drove off. He hoped that would be the end of it. However, in the month that followed, Marilyn made over 250 telephone calls to Bob's work and home, left numerous letters on his car, showed up at his apartment, and started leaving threatening messages for his girlfriend on her answering machine.

Bob contacted the police to obtain a restraining order against Marilyn. About one week after the restraining order was issued, Marilyn attacked Bob's girlfriend with a knife outside her apartment. Bob's girlfriend survived the attack, although she sustained serious injuries. Marilyn was subsequently arrested after being identified by witnesses.

Description of the Borderline Personality

The *Diagnostic and Statistical Manual of Mental Disorders* ([DSM-IV-TR]; American Psychiatric Association, 2000) includes nine items in its description of Borderline Personality Disorder. The items describe three intertwined themes: fragile identity (feelings of emptiness and panic around being alone), emotional instability (volatile mood shifts and intense, inappropriate anger), and behavioral impulsivity (self-damaging behavior and impulsive aggression).

Shapiro's (1952) concept of a "non-factual world" is a good place to start in understanding the borderline personality. For these individuals, nothing is objective or stable, and their mental life is characterized not by thoughts and ideas, but rather by whirlwinds of intensely conflicting emotions. They fear irreversible loss of identity unless a partner is constantly available, but they are unable to relate to that partner in any consistent way, alternating instead between passionate love and overpowering hatred. They have little ability to tolerate frustration without taking some action, and their histories are replete with verbal and physical outbursts, failed relationships, drug and alcohol abuse, and self-harming behavior.

For borderline individuals, there is no stable framework around which to organize their view of themselves or others. Instead, there is constant shifting among opposing emotions in their chaotic world. Borderline individuals operate in extremes, with little ability to adopt a more measured, objective, and perspective-taking stance. At any given moment, they are likely to see themselves as all good or all bad, others as all good or all bad, and the world as a place where they can safely exist or one in which there is only abandonment, pain, and emptiness. They continually move from one extreme to another, based entirely on the circumstances of the moment. Typically, they do not have the impulse control necessary to stop themselves from acting on these extreme emotions, and the result is the pervasive pattern of instability we have described. The only thing that is consistent with borderline individuals is their inconsistency.

From an interpersonal standpoint, the borderline individual vacillates between two equally compelling beliefs: *"My survival depends on having someone in my life"* and *"If I get close to others, they will hurt or abandon me."* The closeness that these individuals crave serves to establish a sense of identity and self-worth that they are unable to develop on their own. They feel as if they can only exist through all-encompassing relationships with others because these relationships provide an escape from feelings of worthlessness, emptiness, and pain. However, the conflict between their need for others and their fear that they will be disappointed, betrayed, or abandoned leads to a repetitive "push-pull" pattern of behavior with devastating consequences.

In summary, the following are core features associated with the borderline personality:

- Unstable and fragile sense of identity (e.g., feelings of emptiness and panic around being alone)
- Emotional instability (e.g., volatile mood shifts and intense, inappropriate anger)
- High level of behavioral impulsivity (e.g., self-damaging behavior and impulsive aggression)
- Extreme and alternating views of self, others, and the world (all good versus all bad)
- Fear of abandonment and constant efforts to avoid it
- A pattern of behavior in relationships marked by intensity, instability, and views of intimate partners/significant others that fluctuate (sometimes rapidly) between extremes of idealization and devaluation

Assessing the Borderline Personality

This section is not designed to exhaust all the sources of information you might use for an indirect assessment of a potential interviewee. Rather, it is designed to suggest a number of questions about the core features of the borderline personality and to offer some suggestions about sources of information typically most useful in answering those questions. Borderline features exist on a continuum. These questions are not for the purpose of diagnosing borderline personality disorder, but rather for determining the presence and intensity of borderline features. Clinically, Borderline Personality Disorder is diagnosed more frequently in women (APA, 2000), and thus we use female pronouns in describing the assessment of these features. However, aspects of this personality occur just as frequently in men, and our suggestions are equally relevant for male interviewees.

The unstable and impulsive features of the borderline individual tend to pervade all aspects of her life but they will typically be most dramatic within intimate relationships. Therefore, current and former partners can often provide specifically useful information. When speaking to them, find out

- When the partner first met the interviewee, did she disclose more personal information than would initially be expected?
- Did she become attached very quickly?
- During the relationship, did she need constant reassurance of being loved and needed?
- Did she idealize the partner when things were going well (e.g., he is the perfect man, their relationship is perfect)?
- Did she quickly become angry and devalue the partner when her needs for constant contact and reassurance were not met? Were her emotions typically intense and constantly shifting between extremes (I love you / I hate you)?
- Did she engage in behaviors that were controlling or made the partner feel she was continually questioning his total concern for her?
- Would he describe her as emotionally volatile? Overall, does she have a history of relationships marked by intense extremes and that tend to begin and end impulsively?

Borderline individuals toward the more severe end of the spectrum can be manipulative, and they often engage in self-harming behaviors or threatening and aggressive actions toward others. Interviews with current or former intimate partners, family members, and friends, as well as a review of medical and criminal records, can often be helpful in this area. Try to determine the following:

- Has she ever threatened suicide?
- Has she ever attempted suicide?
- Does she have a history of substance abuse?

- Has she ever engaged in behaviors designed to "save" a failing relationship (e.g., false claims of pregnancy, false claims of being a victim of a crime, threatening suicide)?
- Has she ever engaged in stalking behaviors?
- Has she ever committed acts of property damage out of anger? Has she ever made threats or been physically aggressive toward others?

These same sources of information can also provide relevant information about childhood and adolescent histories. Clinically, Borderline Personality Disorder is approximately five times more frequent in first-degree family members of those with the disorder (APA, 2000), so a family history, whenever possible, can be useful. Try to obtain the following information:

- Was she ever (or did she ever claim to be) the victim of sexual abuse, physical abuse, or severe emotional abuse?
- Did she ever engage in self-mutilating behaviors (e.g., cutting, burning)?
- Was she sexually promiscuous?
- Did she abuse drugs or alcohol?

Employment and educational histories can also provide valuable information. When asking about her employment or educational background, the following questions may be useful:

- Has she had a history of unstable employment (e.g., moving from job to job)?
- Is there a history of problematic interactions with coworkers or bosses (ranging from verbal altercations to inappropriate sexual relations)?

Again, the borderline personality is best understood as existing on a continuum. Less severe borderline individuals may function adaptively in some areas (e.g., education or employment) and still have significant pathological features, most typically in their interpersonal relationships. For example, if she had the frustration tolerance and self-discipline to achieve any level of secondary education or to maintain consistent employment, she still may have borderline issues within intimate relationships.

Preparation Issues

Preparation is a critical aspect of any interview. This section is intended to provide you with an understanding of those issues that are important considerations as you prepare to interview the borderline individual.

Understanding Your Reactions to the Individual

Before the actual interview begins, you need to be keenly aware of the ways in which you are likely to instinctively respond to the interviewee. Most of the personalities discussed in this book evoke distinct and predictable responses from others. However, because borderline individuals display such a wide range of behavior, you can anticipate the possibility of a wide range of responses. These responses can range from very positive to very negative and can vary dramatically. One minute you may feel anger and a desire to strike back, while the next minute you may find yourself sympathetic and wanting to rescue or help. The instinctive wish to save or rescue (particularly when interviewer and interviewee are of the opposite sex or when the interviewee seems very vulnerable) has the potential for clouding judgment. The interviewee may begin to push boundaries by asking for personal contact information, such as your cell-phone number in case she remembers any additional information. You may find yourself wanting to comply and provide this information. Just be aware that with borderline individuals, this could turn into daily phone calls that have little to do with the case.

Who Should Conduct the Interview

Understanding the interviewee and what the interviewer is likely to encounter is critical in conducting an effective interview. It is equally critical that the interviewer possess the combination of personality traits that make for the best possible outcome.

When possible, it is a goal to establish some level of rapport and trust within the interview process. Working with borderline individuals, it is important for the interviewer to project a level of warmth and sincerity that can help establish that trusting relationship. However, given that borderline individuals tend to quickly attach to others, an empathic and friendly demeanor must be accompanied by the ability to maintain strict professional boundaries. When considering possible interviewers from your department, think of colleagues who people naturally open up to and confide in—someone who demonstrates a calm demeanor and genuine interest in what you are saying. This person should also possess the ability to remain calm, interested, and empathic in the face of drastic changes in temperament, mood, emotion, and rapport.

As always, a thoughtful self-evaluation on the part of the interviewer is crucial. Typically, the law enforcement officer who is assigned the case is likely to conduct the interview. If, however, it is determined that someone else would be better suited, that determination should take precedence in order to increase the likelihood of the interview's success.

Number of Interviewers

The number of interviewers for someone with the borderline personality is not as critical as with some of the other personalities we have discussed. However, because of anxiety issues, there should be one primary interviewer, and the main responsibility of any additional interviewers who are involved should be to take notes.

Physical Space/Environment/Interpersonal Space

For borderline individuals, the initial focus is on reducing anxieties and making every attempt to create a nonthreatening environment. Therefore, consideration should be given to a neutral location that is not imposing, as opposed to a police station. However, if the interview must take place within a law enforcement facility, efforts should be made to bring the individual into the facility and to the room in a way that will not heighten anxiety. For example, bring her in through a side entrance, not in front of a lot of people, and generally refrain from engaging in behaviors that are demeaning (given her already fragile self-esteem).

With regard to interpersonal space, there are several issues to consider. Initially, in order to calm their anxieties, you want to give them appropriately buffered space. Also keep in mind that because of their tendency to attach quickly, borderline individuals (particularly of the opposite sex) may actually invade your personal space as the interview progresses. Therefore, you may want to have some kind of barrier (such as a table or a desk) that allows you the ability to move around. For example, sitting at a forty-five-degree angle across the corner of a table would be one option. While it allows you to move in closer, it also maintains a barrier if needed. Another option would be two chairs facing each other at a distance that allows for adequate personal space.

Nonverbal Behavior

It is recommended that you maintain the kind of eye contact you would typically have in a normal or relaxed conversation with a friend or acquaintance. Appropriate eye contact promotes rapport and establishes connections. This is not the time and place for the kind of prolonged or intense eye contact that can feel challenging in nature. Also, with interviewees of the opposite sex, you want to be careful that you do not engage in body language and eye contact that can be interpreted as suggestive or too intimate.

Questions

The issue with borderline individuals is not so much what questions you ask, but the manner in which you ask them. As noted above, emotions are much more important than facts for individuals with this type of personality. Make every attempt to ask the questions in a subdued, nonthreatening, and nonjudgmental way. A warm, friendly, and understanding approach suggests that you are a stable and trustworthy person.

Recording the Interview (Notetaking, Audio/Video Recording)

If there is more than one interviewer, the primary interviewer can give full attention to the interviewee, and the other interviewer can take notes. For borderline individuals, the primary concern with notetaking is that it does not interfere with the interviewer's ability to give the person his or her complete attention. If you find it necessary to take notes, just explain that you might need to back up and summarize what was said so that you can get some of it down. If you have the ability for audio or video recording with borderline individuals, that would be ideal. By doing this, you can eliminate the need to take notes, making the interview more conversational and informal. In addition, individuals falling toward the disordered end of the borderline continuum may make claims of inappropriate behavior on the part of the interviewer. Video recording of the interview provides a safeguard against such claims.

The Interview

Now that you have a good understanding of the behaviors that borderline individuals are likely to engage in during the interview process and the reasons for those behaviors, settled on an effective interview style, and engaged in thorough preparation, it is time for the actual interview. This section cannot be a comprehensive discussion of all you may encounter, but it will address many of the details that increase the likelihood of the interview going well. In this section we refer to this chapter's opening vignette to emphasize key points made throughout this chapter.

During the initial stages of an interview with borderline individuals, *how* you say things is just as important—and maybe even more important—as *what* you say. Reducing the interviewee's anxiety is the primary goal, and that is best accomplished with reassuring language and a warm, conversational tone.

Interviewer: Hi, Marilyn (delivered in a friendly tone). Is it okay if I call you Marilyn? (Wait for response.) My name is Dan Martin. Can I get you anything before we begin?

The use of the word "Hi," addressing the interviewee by her first name, and the use of a warm, conversational tone are all designed to decrease emotional distance between the interviewer and interviewee.

It is fine to reach out and shake the interviewee's hand. If at all possible, sit down and place yourself at the interviewee's level while talking to her. From the very beginning of the interview, you want to ensure that your body language creates a feeling of openness, warmth, and interest. For example, you do not want to cross your arms, lean away from the interviewee, or engage in any other behavior that makes it appear that you are uninterested or distracted. Think of the interview with the borderline individual as a conversation with a friend you have not seen for a while. Tone, demeanor, and body language all come together to convey the feelings necessary for an open, warm, and non-judgmental environment. Remember that with borderline individuals it is important to strike a balance between creating a warm, open environment and maintaining professional boundaries without being dismissive or critical.

With borderline individuals, you may want to spend more time than usual gathering personal history and background information. Doing this while engaging the interviewee in small talk will help calm anxieties and lay the foundation for developing rapport. In addition, it will allow you to gauge the interviewee's baseline behavior in a nonthreatening environment. This will allow you to quickly identify increases in anxiety, anger, or emotionality as the interview progresses.

As you begin to talk about issues that likely will raise anxiety, structure questions and statements in a way that tells the interviewee you are holding her accountable for her actions while simultaneously expressing interest in what led up to those actions.

Interviewer: Marilyn, as I understand it, you saw your relationship with Bob as special and terribly important to you. I just want to talk to you about how things ended up the way they did. Why don't we start at the beginning? Tell me about how you first met and what happened...

This statement is important for several reasons. First, behavior on the part of the borderline individual is often in response to perceived threats of abandonment or feelings of victimization. As such, empathy on the part of the interviewer is not so much about letting the interviewee know that you feel what she feels, but that you understand *what* she feels and *why*. By using statements like the ones above, you have created an atmosphere where you let her know that the issue at hand is a serious one and that you want to understand what brought her to the point of engaging in some specific behavior. You have created an environment that will allow her to open up and explain her story. You are not condoning her behavior; you are simply saying that you want to understand her actions. You are addressing the crucial issue without being judgmental or confrontational.

Key Points to Remember

Do

- Do be understanding.
- Do be calm, warm, and reassuring in language, tone, and body language.
- Do be open and nonjudgmental.
- Do be conversational.
- Do take your time, particularly at the beginning of the interview.
- Do maintain your composure if the interviewee becomes angry and attacking.
- Do express interest in understanding the person's experience.

Don't

- Don't say, "I know how you feel," or "I understand how you feel," when using empathic statements.
- Don't take a confrontational, authoritative approach.
- Don't be dismissive.
- Don't be condescending.
- Don't allow feelings of wanting to protect and rescue to interfere with the goals of the interview.

References

American Psychiatric Association. (2000). *Diagnostic and statistical manual of mental disorders (4th ed., text rev.).* Washington, DC: American Psychiatric Association.

Shapiro, D. (1965). *Neurotic styles.* New York: Basic Books.

6

THE INADEQUATE/ IMMATURE PERSONALITY

Sarah was excited to get back to college and get away from her overprotective parents. But without her parents, she likely would not have been in college. She was just never able to make a decision about where she wanted to go or what she wanted to study. Her mother actually wrote her college essay and completed all her college applications. Come to think of it, Sarah had difficulty making decisions and functioning independently all her life. Now she was happy that she would not have to deal with her parents asking questions about her social life, and she could do what she wanted without having to answer to anyone. She certainly had a good time her freshman year, partying, drinking with friends, and having the occasional unprotected one-night stand. Several months ago, Sarah had stopped menstruating and was worried about possibly being pregnant. Upon returning to school, she went to the health center for a flu shot and wanted to mention something to the nurse when she was there. However, she had always had irregular cycles and did not think it could actually ever happen to her, so she never brought it up. She bought a pregnancy test a couple of months ago but was too scared to take it, so she just threw it away. Whenever she got worried about being pregnant, she would just take a nap and wish it would all go away. Just the thought of being pregnant would instantly overwhelm her. She would simply tell herself to think about something else. She never told anyone that she thought she might be pregnant because she did not want to disappoint anyone. What would they think of her?

Plus, she was at a Christian school and on an athletic scholarship that she could lose if she was pregnant.

Her roommate, Abby, noticed that Sarah did not go out as much as she used to the previous year and was not drinking anymore. She noticed that Sarah wore large, baggy clothes, even when it was extremely hot. On several occasions, Sarah, who was normally easygoing, was rather short with her and seemed to be moody much of the time. All of Sarah's recent behavioral changes made Abby suspect she might be pregnant. Sarah seemed self-conscious about her weight gain, so Abby was hesitant to confront her. After speaking to several other friends who confirmed they also had the same suspicions, Abby asked Sarah if she was pregnant. Sarah broke down and cried. She knew she had put on some weight and looked awful, but she denied being pregnant. Abby felt awkward about having brought it up and completely dropped the subject.

Three weeks later, Sarah said she was not feeling well and went into the bathroom, where she remained for over an hour. Abby heard the toilet flush several times and the shower running on and off. She also thought she heard Sarah throwing up. Worried, Abby knocked on the door and asked Sarah if she was all right. Sarah peeked out of the door and reassured Abby that she was fine, just having a bad menstrual cycle. Sarah came out a short time later, went into her room, and then went back into the bathroom carrying a trash bag. When she finally came back out, she told her roommate that she was going to the trash room to get rid of the towels she had used to clean up the mess in the bathroom. With everything she had noticed about Sarah's change in behavior, Abby had a sinking suspicion that Sarah may have given birth in the bathroom.

When Sarah returned to the room, she seemed like a totally different person. She was very nonchalant about everything that had just transpired. She was even trying to ask Abby about the homework assignment she was working on. Abby could not concentrate on their conversation and immediately left the room. She went down to the trash room and found the bag that Sarah had placed there. Abby hesitantly opened the bag, cautiously moved the bloody towels, and saw an infant's foot at the bottom of the trash bag. Screaming hysterically, she ran from the room and called 911 from her cell phone.

Description of the Inadequate/Immature Personality

When discussing the inadequate/immature personality, we are essentially merging the inadequate and emotionally unstable personality patterns described in the first edition of the *Diagnostic and Statistical Manual of Mental Disorders* ([DSM-I]; American Psychiatric Association, 1952). Some of the core characteristics of these two personality patterns include significant difficulty responding to intellectual, emotional, social, or physical demands, particularly in stressful or complicated situations. Judgment is typically not good, and these individuals have poor stamina, both physically and emotionally. They also have poor interpersonal skills. They react with excitability and ineffective responses when confronted with even minor stress. Overall, these individuals do not adapt well to their changing environments, often becoming overwhelmed with responses that are inept and inefficient.

These are individuals who, despite adequate intellectual ability, continually do not meet the standards or expectations of someone their age. They are passive and rely on others to make decisions for them. They do not take the lead in solving problems, instead depending on others for guidance. They also have very little self-awareness or insight into their behavior. When asked why they did something, they may answer with a response such as, "I don't know" and really mean it. They can easily become overwhelmed by daily life. When this occurs, they simply retreat from reality into a fantasy world. As a result of this type of defensive functioning, they often lack long-term goals and lead a life without direction. Due to their inability to delay gratification, they often appear childlike with their impatient and impulsive behavior. Given their lack of insight and awareness, they frequently fail to consider the consequences of the behavior in which they engage.

These individuals often seem emotionally unstable, as they may experience frequent mood swings. They have an emotional fragility with little control over their emotions, again making them seem rather child-like. These individuals do not consider the entire situation before making a judgment, and they can be easily influenced by someone they have just met.

In summary, inadequate/immature individuals exhibit the following features:

- They are emotionally fragile
- They are unable to delay gratification
- They are easily overwhelmed
- They often do not see the long-term consequences of their behavior
- They rely heavily on others for guidance
- They vacillate between emotions
- They are easily influenced
- They are often rather passive
- They lack decision-making skills
- They have limited self-awareness
- They lack mature judgment
- They can be impulsive
- They have poor interpersonal skills

Assessing the Inadequate/Immature Personality

This section is not designed to exhaust all sources of information that you can utilize to conduct an indirect assessment of a potential interviewee. Rather, it is designed to provide a number of questions that address the core features of the inadequate/immature personality discussed throughout this chapter and to offer some suggestions regarding sources of information typically most useful in answering those questions. Remember that these questions are *not* for the purpose of diagnosing the interviewee, but rather for determining the presence and strength of the inadequate/immature features of his or her personality. For the purposes of clarity, this section is written for the assessment of a female interviewee, but the ideas presented would be just as relevant for a male interviewee.

One of the central features of the inadequate/immature personality is the inability to respond appropriately to stressful situations and the lack of judgment demonstrated within these settings. Therefore, when interviewing family and friends, you may want to explore the following questions:

- Is she easily overwhelmed by daily tasks?
- Does she seem to exhibit poor judgment?
- Does she have poor decision-making skills?
- Does she seem to lack any long-term goals?
- Does she often let others make important decisions for her?
- Does she have intense feelings of inadequacy and helplessness?
- Does she suffer from low confidence?
- Does she have difficulty making decisions without reassurance from others?
- Does she seem to avoid personal responsibility?
- Is she unable to meet the ordinary demands of life?

Inadequate/immature individuals tend to struggle in close relationships with others due to their emotional fragility and lack of interpersonal maturity. When interviewing others, try to find out what the inadequate/immature individual's attitudes and behaviors are regarding relationships:

- Is she extremely passive in her relationships with other people?
- Does she not take responsibility for her behaviors or actions within a relationship?
- Does she feel devastated or helpless when a relationship ends?
- Does she seem emotionally unstable?
- Does she lack emotional maturity?
- Does she seem more childlike in her relationships with others?
- Does she seem to let others make decisions for her?
- Are her problem-solving abilities below that of her peers?

Preparation Issues

Preparation is a critical aspect of any interview. The intent of this section is to provide you with an understanding of those issues that are important considerations as you prepare to interview the inadequate/immature individual.

Understanding Your Reactions to the Individual

Before conducting the interview, it is important to be keenly aware of the instinctive ways in which you are likely to respond to the interviewee. As you approach an interview with inadequate/immature individuals, you may initially be pleasantly surprised by how cooperative and attentive they are. They can be rather people-pleasing and want to provide you with all the information you are requesting. They will likely remain cooperative until the interviewer begins to hold them accountable for their behavior or asks questions that require a more adult-like approach to problem solving. Because these individuals tend to avoid personal responsibility and lack emotional maturity, they will likely struggle with seeing a connection between their behavior and its consequences.

You may soon feel frustrated, and perhaps even angry, by the interviewee's inability to take responsibility for her own behavior. Despite her age, she reasons and makes judgments with the decision-making power of a child. You may find yourself wanting to help her connect the dots as to how her behavior influenced the outcome. However, this can be a challenging task and will likely result in a lack of cooperation rather than increased self-awareness.

Who Should Conduct the Interview

Understanding the interviewee is critical to conducting an effective interview. It is equally critical that the interviewer possess the combination of personality traits that will support an effective interview style. Because these individuals are childlike in their emotions and thoughts, it is best to select an interviewer who will come across as a parental figure. This will provide a more familiar and comfortable environment for the inadequate/immature person who relies on others (often parents) to help them through the stressors of life. Because they often feel overwhelmed and incapable of handling even minor demands, the interviewer should be someone who presents as genuine, competent, and caring. The interviewer should also be someone who can provide an empathic interview setting. This will help set the tone of the actual interview.

In addition, the interviewer should be someone who is patient and can tolerate the inadequate/immature individual's lack of responsibility and accountability for his or her actions. In this way, when faced with the individual's inability to cope or problem-solve, the interviewer can empathically acknowledge the interviewee's response to the situation.

As always, a thoughtful, honest self-evaluation on the part of the interviewer is crucial. Typically, the law enforcement officer assigned to the case is likely to conduct the interview. If, however, it is determined that someone else would be better suited to conduct the interview, that determination should take precedence in order to increase the likelihood of the interview's success.

Number of Interviewers

The number of interviewers for this type of personality is less critical than for the other personalities discussed in this book. The more important issue is the sense of supportive parental competence that the interviewer brings to the meeting. If there are two interviewers, one should be designated the primary interviewer while the second should be solely responsible for taking notes. The second interviewer's role should be discussed with the interviewee. We would strongly discourage involving more than two interviewers to prevent the interviewee from feeling intimidated.

Physical Space/Environment/Interpersonal Space

For inadequate/immature individuals, it is important that everything in the environment convey a sense of comfort. Therefore, you may want to set up the room without a table in between the interviewer and the interviewee, allowing for closer personal space. This is in contrast to many of the other disorders discussed in this book, as we noted that invading personal space might be anxiety provoking. However, with these individuals, just as they look to others for guidance and emotional stability, they will look to the interviewer to help guide them through the interview. Because they lack emotional and intellectual sophistication, closer physical proximity will help provide that comfort level.

Inadequate/immature individuals will likely seek reassurance from the interviewer. Think of these individuals as very childlike. It is recommended that you provide them with the types of physical and emotional support that will keep them comfortable in the interview environment and keep them talking. For instance, the interviewer may want to frequently ask how they are doing. Do they need to take a break? Are they hungry? How are they feeling? Are they getting tired? These types of questions demonstrate an inherent care-taking and nurturing quality that will help the inadequate/immature individual feel more comfortable. While this may seem counterintuitive, helping inadequate/immature individuals feel more comfortable should increase your chances of a productive interview.

Nonverbal Behavior

These individuals are not overly sophisticated or focused on subtleties within their environments. Given their limited self-awareness and immaturity, they are not overly in tune with others, and are inexperienced and underdeveloped in reading other people. That being said, it is important to communicate and convey openness in your nonverbal behavior. Sitting with your arms folded across your chest at a distance from interviewees may make them feel abandoned and judged. These are individuals who will respond positively to eye contact, leaning forward, and head nodding while they are talking. All of these nonverbal behaviors bring an empathic tone to the interview.

Questions

It is recommended that you take the time to write out some questions that you will need to address during the course of the interview. By actually writing out some of these questions, it may help to eliminate any judgmental component. These interviews should be approached in an empathic, nurturing, and nonjudgmental manner. Having an idea of the actual questions you want to ask prior to the interview may help minimize any underlying biases. For example, when approaching the interview with Sarah, the interviewer will want to explore her visit to the university's health services nurse. The interviewer may be more successful in obtaining information about this visit by empathizing with Sarah about not feeling well, being away from home, and still needing to keep up with college-level academic demands. Then the interviewer may ask whether the nurse inquired about any other health conditions or if any lab work was conducted, as opposed to a more confrontational or judgmental question such as asking why she did not tell the nurse she was pregnant. Remember that these individuals do not see the long-term consequences of their behaviors, so it is possible that Sarah did not see any connection between being evaluated by a health professional and not revealing that she was pregnant.

Keep in mind that the manner in which questions are asked is almost as important as the questions themselves. The interviewer needs to ask questions in an empathic manner that conveys a desire to help. This approach will be familiar, as these individuals have been provided with help and guidance throughout their lives.

Recording the Interview (Notetaking, Audio/Video Recording)

Notetaking is always recommended to help pace the interview and allow the interviewer to identify areas that he or she may need to further explore. Inadequate/immature individuals are less sensitive to their environments than other personalities who are more vigilant and concerned about potential threats. These inadequate/immature individuals are looking for guidance and care from others and would likely not question the presence or purpose of notetaking.

Audio and video recording is recommended. It should be addressed as a matter of policy in order to ensure the accuracy of the interview for the protection of the interviewee. Regardless of whether you use audio or video recording, notetaking is still recommended for the aforementioned reasons.

Time Frame

The time frame for the interview should accommodate the comfort aspects that may be necessary to sustain the interview. Again, these individuals will likely be cooperative and helpful in providing the requested information. The interview will take on a challenging twist when these individuals are questioned about their inability to see the consequences of their behavior, their passivity, and their overall lack of self-awareness. It may take time to sort through this part of the interview. Overall, these individuals will respond to a supportive and helpful interviewer.

The Interview

Now that you have a good understanding of the behaviors inadequate/immature individuals are likely to engage in and the reasons for those behaviors, settled on an effective interview style, and engaged in thorough preparation, it is time for the actual interview. This section cannot be a comprehensive summary of everything you might encounter, but it will address many of the details that increase the likelihood of the interview going well. In this section we use the vignette of Sarah presented earlier to emphasize the key points.

Inadequate/immature individuals lack stamina and self-awareness, and have little concept of responsibility; therefore they often feel the need to be guided and cared for by others. You want to set the tone for a successful interview, which means creating an environment where they feel comfortable and are willing to talk about the details of their behavior. A good way to establish this setting is by beginning the interview in a manner that lays the foundation and tone for how the interview will proceed. Start by introducing yourself. Using your name and title may actually help to further reinforce that you are someone they can trust as you clearly hold a position of authority. That being said, if you are a homicide detective, you may not want to mention the unit to which you are assigned. Also, you may want to shake hands with the inadequate/immature individual. By having this initial personal contact, it may suggest a degree of warmth and connectedness that they will need to sustain them throughout the course of the interview. Consider the following example in the case of Sarah:

Interviewer: My name is Detective Dan Martin and I am with the local Police Department. You're Sarah, right? Is it okay if I call you Sarah?

Sarah: Yes.

Interviewer: Great. We'll probably be talking for a while Sarah; so before we get started, is there anything I can get for you? Coffee? Soda? Also, if you need to use the bathroom, just let me know and we can take a break.

While this level of concern may feel counterintuitive, it is important because thoughtful caretaking helps inadequate/immature individuals feel safe and secure. Again, while it is difficult to think of these individuals as childlike because they are adults, you need to show them the same care and concern you would a child. So, in this example, by asking Sarah if she is thirsty or needs to use the bathroom, you are addressing those basic concerns that will help her feel cared for and more comfortable within an unfamiliar environment. Also, using her name frequently will help make things more personal. These initial strategies will result in the inadequate/immature individual feeling comfortable enough to talk, which is the ultimate goal of the interview.

Another core feature of inadequate/immature individuals is their emotional and intellectual immaturity and fragility. An empathic interview style is recommended to show care and concern on the part of the interviewer. By acknowledging their feelings, you are not judging interviewees, but rather aligning with them. For example, in the case of the neonaticide vignette with Sarah, many interviewers might want to take a hard-line approach, such as

Interviewer: It seems you clearly suspected, if not knew for sure, that you were pregnant. Why didn't you do something?

Sarah: I just didn't know what to do? (crying)

Interviewer: How could you not know what to do? You're a college student. You even went to health services for a cold. Why wouldn't you tell the nurse that you were pregnant?

Sarah: I don't know why I didn't tell anyone ... I was afraid (still crying).

As demonstrated by this example, Sarah is being challenged and the interviewer is clearly expecting her to have adult-like decision-making and problem-solving skills for dealing with a difficult situation. However, this approach is not resulting in Sarah saying anything more than that she does not know why she did what she did. As an alternative, consider the following empathic approach:

Interviewer: Sarah, I'm going to ask you some questions that I know might be tough for you to answer, but I need your full cooperation, okay?

Sarah: Okay, I'll try.

Interviewer: Good. So you mentioned that you thought you might be pregnant but that your menstrual cycles weren't always consistent, so you weren't sure. At any point, did you take a pregnancy test?

Sarah: Yes, but I threw it away.

Interviewer: It sounds like you were scared.

Sarah: Of course I was scared. I was afraid my roommates might find the pregnancy test so I wrapped it in a tee-shirt and threw it away in the trash room on the floor of our dorm.

This example helps demonstrate that simply commenting on how she might have been feeling at the time rather than accusing her or judging her behavior may lead to a more productive response. This, in turn, results in her providing more detailed information rather than her simply retreating and disengaging from the interview and saying she does not know.

You may also recall that inadequate/immature individuals lack long-term planning and the ability to anticipate the consequences of their behavior. Therefore, the interviewer may be inclined to ask Sarah the following questions:

Interviewer: If you suspected you were pregnant, what was your plan for handling the pregnancy?

Sarah: I just hoped it would go away.

Interviewer: And you thought that would work?

It would be tempting to follow this line of questioning, given the fact that this was a situation that clearly required some plan of action. But that is exactly the point. These capabilities are what the inadequate/immature individual does not have. Engaging in this line of questioning would be an exercise in futility. Another way of approaching the same issue might be the following:

Interviewer: If you suspected you were pregnant, how did you deal with that for so long?
Sarah: I just hoped it would go away.
Interviewer: It seems like it made you anxious.
Sarah: Exactly. I would feel so anxious that I just got so tired and couldn't think about it anymore.
Interviewer: Did you tell anyone?
Sarah: No, I just couldn't bring myself to. I was afraid that they would judge me.

Here you are asking the same types of questions, but as opposed to confronting her lack of long-term planning, you comment on how she would likely feel because she had no plan. This would be a more effective approach than identifying her weakness.

Another approach with Sarah would be to empathize with how she must have been feeling as this situation was unfolding. Again, although it may seem counterintuitive, this nonaccusatory approach, as in the following example, is often the best way to keep the interview going productively:

Interviewer: Sarah, I'd like to talk with you a bit more about the time you were in your dorm bathroom. It seems like there was a lot going on at that time. It had to be very frightening for you.
Sarah: Yeah, it was frightening but I think I was more scared during my pregnancy. When I was in the bathroom, I knew I just had to get through it and everything would be okay. I just kept thinking about my softball scholarship and how I could lose everything.
Interviewer: That had to be very overwhelming for you.

Sarah: I just couldn't think about it all. I would start to and then I'd get so tired. I'd just lie down and take a nap and hope it would all go away.

This example demonstrates the approach of empathizing with the person you are interviewing. Rather than focusing on the baby (or even mentioning the baby at all), your focus is about how overwhelmed Sarah was at the time of the offense. While you will undoubtedly have strong personal emotions about the offense, realizing that this is a tragedy for everyone and empathizing with the interviewee can be an effective strategy for individuals who are limited in their capacity to appreciate the consequences of their behavior. By referring to her emotions at the time of the offense as "frightening" and "overwhelming," you reinforce what she was experiencing and increase the chances of eliciting detailed information.

Overall, when interviewing inadequate/immature individuals, it is best to keep your expectations consistent with their abilities. Remind yourself that while it may appear that there is an adult with you in the room, the inadequate/immature individual functions at a more child-like level. If you maintain those expectations and approach the interview in an empathic manner, you will likely have a more productive result.

Key Points to Remember

Do

- Do be extremely patient.
- Do be empathic and understanding.
- Do be comforting and nurturing.
- Do provide guidance and reassurance.

Don't

- Don't be judgmental.
- Don't be distant.
- Don't be overly aggressive or direct.

Reference

American Psychiatric Association. (1952). *Diagnostic and statistical manual of mental disorders (1st edition)*. Washington, DC: American Psychiatric Association.

7

THE PARANOID PERSONALITY

Paul Jones arrived at 7:30 a.m. at the large construction company where he worked, about a half hour early, as usual. He entered the building and gave the obligatory "Good morning" as he walked past a few coworkers. He sat down at his desk and, as he waited for his computer to power up, looked carefully around the office. Noticing that a couple of things seemed out of place, Paul immediately headed toward his supervisor's office and went on the offensive, demanding to know who had been in his office. As a mechanical engineer, Paul was accustomed to working by himself and liked it that way. So, in his mind, there was really no reason for anyone to have been in his office, digging through his things. His supervisor, Greg, recognizing Paul's tendency to be suspicious and aggressive, calmly explained that he and another manager had worked late the night before and needed a file from Paul's office. Greg assured him that that was all they needed and that they would never look into his personal items. With that explanation, Paul left and returned to his office. He was very upset that they had opened his file cabinet when he wasn't there, invading his personal space.

As he walked back down the hallway, he saw some coworkers talking. As he approached, he heard them laughing and joking. He confronted them and asked if they were laughing about him. His coworkers assured him that their laughter had nothing to do with him. Agitated, he walked into his office and shut the door. He was not close with any of his coworkers. He worried that they were likely to take advantage of him.

Later, Paul's supervisor (Greg) called him into his office and informed him that his wages were going to be garnished because he was delinquent in his alimony and child support payments. Paul responded angrily, saying that his ex-wife "turned on me and now she's got everyone taking her side." Greg explained that the company did not have any choice in the matter in the face of a court order. Paul went on to say, "This is the last straw. I've done everything I could. I've made phone calls and written letters to the judge and to my congressman about how unfair this is. I'm sick of being the victim and now you're like everybody else; you're just out to get me. You're on their side too." Greg told Paul to take the day off to relax and cool down. Paul got up and stormed out of the office.

The next day Paul sent in his letter of resignation. From then on, he continued to write letters to his former place of employment, the judge, government agencies, and anyone else he could think of to resolve the situation to his satisfaction.

Six months later, a package containing a pipe bomb was mailed to the company where Paul had worked; it was addressed to his supervisor, Greg. The package was opened by an administrative assistant, detonating the bomb and causing severe injury.

Description of the Paranoid Personality

The *Diagnostic and Statistical Manual of Mental Disorders* ([DSM-IV-TR]; American Psychiatric Association, 2000) includes seven items in its description of Paranoid Personality Disorder, but they are all variations on a single theme: pervasive distrust. The paranoid individual is endlessly on the alert because he or she expects to be exploited in an interpersonal world that is full of danger. There is constant questioning of others' loyalty, and the paranoid individual sees hidden meanings and conspiracies behind the most innocuous comments. Easily slighted, these individuals are terribly sensitive to criticism, and the grudges they hold extend across months, years, and decades. They need to remain in a continuous state of vigilant mobilization against threat, and they often feel that the best defense is a good offense.

Shapiro (1965) identifies an important feature of this pervasively distrusting style. Paranoid individuals constantly look for confirmation of their fixed belief that the world is a dangerous place set on betraying them, and they ignore any indications to the contrary. These individuals do not pay attention to contradictory information, dismissing anything that does not confirm their suspicions and seizing on anything that does. As Shapiro (1965) puts it, "...the underlying truth invariably turns out to be precisely what they expected it to be in the first place" (p. 56).

Given a worldview of unremitting interpersonal danger and threat, you might think that paranoid individuals would decide to limit their contacts with others and withdraw. But the paradox is that these individuals work hard to stay connected, although in increasingly maladaptive ways. Auchincloss and Weiss (1992) provide an explanation for this seemingly contradictory behavior. They suggest that paranoid individuals have had some positive interpersonal connections and continue to need relationships. But perhaps because of some negative experiences, they are unable to assume that others will be reliably and supportively available. Unable to make a needed attachment at an emotional level and faced with the intolerable prospect of no attachment at all, paranoid individuals use thinking as a way of staying connected. They constantly think about others and imagine that others are thinking about them, using ideation to replace the connections they cannot create emotionally. But ultimately the idea that others are constantly thinking about them collides with another basic human necessity: the need for privacy. Auchincloss and Weiss (1992) suggest that paranoid individuals are in a bind: they cannot feel connected unless they assume that others are thinking about them, but that assumption increasingly leads to concerns that others will use the information they gather in harmful and intrusive ways. Ultimately, these fears consolidate and lead to the threatening worldview we have described.

As individuals move toward the severe end of the paranoid spectrum, they increasingly look at others as intrusive, malicious, and deceptive. They are constantly alert for signs of danger and interpret any slightly ambiguous communication or behavior as confirmation of their suspicions. They ignore nothing that others say or do and they keep track of everything. A cold, distant, and humorless demeanor is their shield against emotional closeness, which, to their way of thinking, would only give others the chance to betray or harm them. They try to control their environment because, by doing so, they reduce the likelihood of danger. Interpersonal situations in which they have little or no control represent figurative "mine fields" of potential danger. They project an image of independence and strength because appearing weak or vulnerable only encourages others to take advantage of them. Believing that attacks are inevitable, they may engage in unprovoked aggressive, contentious, or hostile behavior as a sort of preemptive strike.

One of the by-products of their projection of negative attributes onto others is that it leaves paranoid individuals with robustly virtuous self-concepts. Truly believing themselves to be the victims of intentional attempts to harm them, they respond, sometimes aggressively, with an unshakable sense of justice and righteousness.

In summary, the following are core features associated with the paranoid personality:

- A sense of distrust and suspiciousness that pervades all aspects of their lives
- A general view of others as untrustworthy, malicious, and deceptive
- A view of the world as hostile and dangerous
- A constant hypervigilance to signs of danger and deception
- A continual interpretation of even minimal or ambiguous data as evidence to support his or her suspicions
- An avoidance of developing close relationships and keeping an emotional distance from others
- A tendency to keep track of perceived injustices
- Continually engaging in controlling behaviors to minimize risks or threats to themselves
- A serious, humorless demeanor
- Often acting in aggressive or hostile ways
- Constantly mobilized in a "fight or flight" state
- A view of the world as "black or white," or in terms of extremes (e.g., good versus evil, right versus wrong)

- Perceiving and experiencing things in extremes (e.g., there is no such thing as a slight criticism)
- Tendency to view their behaviors as righteous or justified

Assessing the Paranoid Personality

This section is not designed to summarize all the sources of information you might draw on for an indirect assessment of a potential interviewee. Rather, it is designed to suggest a number of questions focused on the core features of paranoid personality disorder and to offer some suggestions regarding sources of information typically most useful in answering those questions. Paranoid features exist on a continuum ranging from mild to severe. These questions are not for the purpose of diagnosing the interviewee with paranoid personality disorder, but rather for determining the presence and intensity of paranoid features. Clinically, Paranoid Personality Disorder is more frequently diagnosed in men (APA, 2000), and we have used masculine pronouns in describing the assessment of this personality. However, our suggestions are just as relevant for assessing paranoid features in women.

- First and foremost, determine whether he has a pervasive level of distrust that impacts how he functions in all aspects of his life. Does he tend to be distrustful or suspicious in multiple contexts? For paranoid individuals, their deep level of distrust has wide-ranging interpersonal implications. Ask others if he constantly demands assurances of loyalty. Does he frequently accuse others of disloyalty? Do others describe him as paranoid?
- Another area to consider is interpersonal warmth, which can be addressed through a few simple questions as well. Would others describe him as cold and distant? Does he currently have any close friends, or did he during childhood or adolescence? Does he confide in others? Do people who know him seem to like him? Would people say that he rarely laughs or smiles?
- Find out whether he has issues with frustration and anger. Is he easily frustrated? Is his anger disproportionate to the situation? Does he become aggressive and confrontational at those

times? Paranoid individuals tend to provoke anger and hostility in others in ways that validate what they already believe. Finding out if his behavior provokes these responses provides useful information.

- Another critical issue is sensitivity to slights, humiliation, and criticism. Does he tend to forgive and forget easily, or does he hold grudges? Is he constantly misinterpreting words and actions as hostile or malicious? Although the relationship is a modest one, there is some suggestion that paranoid individuals are more likely to have family members with delusional disorders of the persecutory type (APA, 2000). Try to find out whether he tends to think in terms of extremes. Would others describe him as very concrete and dogmatic with an all-or-nothing style of thinking? Is he very judgmental and dismissive?

- With paranoid individuals, another important place to gather information is through records review. Many of these individuals choose legal means for addressing grievances. They often engage in letter writing and lawsuits to fight against perceived slights. Therefore, a review of civil and criminal records is useful. Has he filed any civil suits? Has he been the subject of any criminal complaints, particularly in areas such as harassment? Has he filed any criminal complaints against others (e.g., harassment, trespassing)?

- If you find that others say that loyalty is of supreme importance to him; that he has relatively few close friends, if any; that he is distrustful of authority; that at times he reacts in a hostile manner to benign situations without provocation; or that he holds grudges for long periods, then you have identified some of the core features of the paranoid personality.

Preparation Issues

Preparation is a critical aspect of any interview. The intent of this section is to provide you with an understanding of those issues that are important considerations as you prepare to interview the paranoid individual.

Understanding Your Reactions to the Individual

Before conducting the interview, it is important to be keenly aware of the instinctive ways in which you are likely to respond to a paranoid interviewee. These individuals present a twofold problem in that they enter the interview with deep-rooted and enduring beliefs that are then confirmed by the law enforcement context. Within the interview setting, the paranoid individual's maladaptive beliefs likely center around assumptions such as "I can't trust the interviewer," or "I know the interviewer wants to harm me." The individual assumes hostile intent and views the interviewer's actions as nothing more than attempts to attack, trick, harm, or deceive. Even with all your attempts to keep the setting low-key and neutral, their already high level of anxiety may be heightened and they may cling even more tightly to their maladaptive beliefs and behaviors. As such, it is not uncommon for a paranoid individual to be verbally aggressive and adopt a demeanor that can be angry, hostile, sarcastic, condescending, or accusatory. Faced with the resistant, contentious, and provocative behavior that stems from paranoid beliefs, it is understandable that any interviewer's instinct would be to respond with irritation, anger, or defensiveness. But that response would confirm what the paranoid individual already believes, shutting down the interview almost before it begins. While the interviewee may not immediately engage in such behavior, you need to anticipate its possibility. Awareness of this potential will help you to not respond defensively to the individual's attacks and accusations, instead maintaining a neutral stance that keeps the interview on track.

Remember: *do not take it personally.* The attacks and accusations are the product of what law enforcement represents in the individual's belief system. If you take it personally, you will not be able to prevent your irritation and defensiveness from showing. Once you let that happen, you will have validated the interviewee's negative expectations and significantly lowered the likelihood of a productive interview.

Another issue to be prepared for during interviews is the tendency for paranoid individuals to place the blame for unacceptable behavior on others, sometimes even the victim. Anyone would find this kind of blaming—particularly if the victim is a child—to be reprehensible. Therefore, it is important that the interviewer be aware of the instinctively angry response that such behavior is likely to provoke. Controlling such a response, even when an interviewee rationalizes intolerable behavior by diverting responsibility to a vulnerable victim, ensures that the interview will succeed in gathering the information necessary to move the law enforcement process to the next step.

Who Should Conduct the Interview

Understanding the interviewee is critical to conducting an effective interview. It is equally critical that the interviewer possess the combination of personality traits that will support an effective interview style. Typically, one of the goals during the interview process is to establish some level of rapport and trust. However, because of the pervasive distrust that is central to the paranoid personality, that is unlikely to happen. Instead, the initial goal when interviewing individuals with paranoid features is to respond to their anxiety and apprehension in ways that do not heighten their level of mistrust.

First and foremost, it is essential that the interviewer is someone who is capable of remaining calm in the face of the strong negative feelings that the interviewee is likely to communicate. An interviewer who becomes defensive, is quick to anger, or tends to be emotional will only reinforce the interviewee's expectations. In addition to an even temperament, it is equally important that the interviewer convey a sense of professionalism and sincerity. However, he or she must be careful to communicate sincere professionalism without appearing overly friendly. Boundary issues are absolutely critical, and any sense that the interviewer is violating those boundaries by being too friendly can be misinterpreted by the interviewee as an attempt to trick him.

Another consideration is the manner in which the interviewer asks questions. As noted above, paranoid individuals interpret ambiguous remarks or actions as supportive of their beliefs. An interviewer who asks questions or makes statements that are lengthy and complex will create an interview environment rich with ambiguity. Instead, questions and statements should be clear and concise, lowering the likelihood that the interviewee can interpret or distort them.

When talking about interview styles, it is important to discuss the empathic approach in relation to paranoid individuals. Empathy communicates a sharing of emotional experience between individuals. One of the things law enforcement officers learn in interview training is how important empathy typically is in developing trust and rapport. However, the use of an empathic approach with paranoid individuals can be problematic. These individuals may view an empathic approach much the same way they view friendliness: as an attempt to trick or deceive. If the interviewer decides to utilize empathic statements, they should be infrequent, strategically placed, and specific to an experience the interviewee has reported. You do not want to use empathic statements, such as, "I know how you feel," or "I understand how you feel." Empathic statements, such as, "When that happened, it sounds like it made you angry," have the most potential for being effective.

As always, a thoughtful, honest self-evaluation on the part of the interviewer is crucial. Typically, the law enforcement officer assigned to the case is likely to conduct the interview. If, however, it is determined that someone else would be better suited to conduct the interview, that determination should take precedence in order to increase the likelihood of the interview's success.

Number of Interviewers

Limit the number of interviewers to no more than two. A primary interviewer should conduct the interview with the second officer there to take notes. It is recommended that the second interviewer not interrupt or ask questions, as that disrupts the flow and structure of the interview.

Physical Space/Environment/Interpersonal Space

With paranoid individuals, issues of power and authority are always at the forefront. For that reason, you may want to hold the interview, if at all possible, in a neutral location, so as not to heighten the hypervigilant state these individuals always bring to a new situation. A neutral location is one that gives neither the investigator nor the suspect greater authority in ways that a police station might for an investigator or the person's home might for a suspect. Consider a location that presents as little chance as possible for misinterpretation. If you have access to an off-site setting that has no connection to power or authority, that would be ideal.

However, if the individual is in custody, or if an interrogation is planned (or a possibility), then the interview will most likely be held in a law enforcement or correctional facility. Just remember that the setting and everything in it (flags, uniforms, etc.) all represent power and authority to the paranoid individual, and consideration should be given to bringing the person into the interview room in as unthreatening a way as possible. For example, you may want to bring the person in through a less-imposing side or back door, where you pass fewer people, and into a room void of anything that represents power, authority, or unnecessary stimuli. The same principles apply for off-site settings. You want them to be low-key and as "sterile" as possible.

With paranoid individuals, interpersonal and physical space considerations go hand in hand. These individuals do not want their space invaded physically, visually, or emotionally. It is recommended that the room setup be such that there is space around them during the interview. These individuals do not want to be deprived of their "buffer zones" (Shea, 1998). A desk or table between the interviewer and the interviewee provides the necessary space. Invading the personal space of a paranoid individual is perceived as threatening, and the natural response to threat is "fight or flight," causing the interviewee to become aggressive or retreat into silence (or worse, terminate the interview). Another important point about visual space is that if two interviewers are involved, each should be equally visible, with neither in the background.

Nonverbal Behavior

The interviewer should strive to maintain body language that conveys openness and professionalism, but not intimacy. One issue that is important with paranoid individuals is eye contact. Under ordinary circumstances, eye contact is seen as an indication of sincerity, openness, honesty, genuineness, and interest. However, paranoid individuals may interpret sustained eye contact as confrontational or adversarial. An interviewer may consider periodically breaking eye contact because prolonged eye contact can be misinterpreted as an attempt at intimidation (Shea, 1998).

Questions

It is highly recommended that the interviewer script out the questions that will be asked during the interview. This accomplishes a number of objectives. First, it will allow you to check that your questions are brief and unambiguous. Second, it will allow you to plan the structure of the interview. This ensures that you ask all the necessary questions in a clear and logical manner. This will also help you to stay on track, without losing focus and better able to handle deviations when they occur. Also, with scripted questions, you are less likely to ask an ambiguous question that can be misinterpreted by the interviewee. You do not need to memorize the questions; however, they should be practiced enough that you can move from one to the next in a very deliberate yet natural way. Remember that it is not just what you say, but how you say it. You want everything that you say and do in the interview to convey a sense of quiet professionalism, competence, and respect.

Recording the Interview (Notetaking, Audio/Video Recording)

If at all possible, neither interviewer should take notes during the initial stage of the interview. The goal of this part of the interview is to manage anxiety, using the time to explain the structure of the interview and establish a professional tone. Once this introduction is completed, it of course becomes necessary to take notes, an integral part of law enforcement interviews. To minimize misinterpretation of the notetaking, it is important to be straightforward with the interviewee, explaining that careful notetaking is one way the law enforcement process ensures accuracy. As recommended above, we suggest that a second individual take the notes.

Paranoid individuals are exquisitely sensitive to detail, and thus notetaking should be continuous, not just limited to times when the information seems important to the interviewer(s). If you decide (or are required) to have audio or video recording, it should be addressed up front and in a straightforward way as a standard part of the interview process and a tool for ensuring accuracy. If you do utilize audio or video to record the interview, it is probably best that you do not also take notes. However, the decision as to whether to take notes at this point is an issue of personal style and whether you feel it enhances your ability to conduct an effective interview. If you decide to take notes, then do so in the manner previously discussed. One more point regarding audio and video recording is worth mentioning here: If you do not intend to use these procedures, then, if at all possible, conduct the interview in a room free of cameras or other recording equipment. If there is a camera (or some other recording device) in the room, you can rest assured that paranoid individuals will spot it and automatically assume that you are using this equipment. Trying to convince them that the equipment is not being used will be difficult, if not impossible.

Time Frame

Given that the core feature of Paranoid Personality Disorder is extreme distrust, your goal is not to establish rapport but to create an environment where the person does not feel threatened. This can take some time. Therefore, if the interviewer has the luxury, then he or she may want to divide the interview into a couple of sessions.

The Interview

Now that you have a good understanding of the behaviors that paranoid individuals are likely to engage in during the interview process and the reasons for those behaviors, settled on an effective interview style, and engaged in thorough preparation, it is time for the actual interview. This section cannot be a comprehensive discussion of all that you might encounter, but it does address many of the details that increase the likelihood of the interview going well. In this section we refer to the opening vignette to emphasize key points made throughout the chapter.

The interview itself begins with the introductory process, which should set a straightforward, professional tone. You should begin by greeting the interviewee in a professional manner and then ask how he would prefer to be addressed.

Interviewer: Good morning, sir. Shall I call you Mr. Jones, or would you prefer something else?

At first glance, this may seem like a rather insignificant point. However, greeting the paranoid individual in this manner and asking how he would like to be addressed accomplishes several objectives. First, it sets the tone of respect and professionalism you are seeking, while, at the same time maintaining the emotional distance that the paranoid individual needs. When you address someone by a first name, it reduces emotional distance. Think of the phrase, "We are on a first-name basis." It implies friendship and closeness. Reducing emotional distance with paranoid individuals, particularly early in the interview, runs the risk of creating discomfort and raising anxiety. Second, asking how he or would like to be addressed allows the paranoid individual an initial sense of control.

Continuing on with the introductory process, you should introduce yourself by first and last name. In addition, provide a brief, straightforward overview of the interview process through the use of nonconfrontational and nonemotional language.

Interviewer: Good morning, sir. Shall I call you Mr. Jones, or would you prefer something else? My name is Dan Martin and I am working on the AmeriCon case. The purpose of this interview is to talk with you about your knowledge of the events of August 16th. I would like to begin by obtaining some background information from you. After that, I'd like to ask you some specific questions regarding the events of that day.

By not using your professional title, which represents the power of your agency and the government in general, you avoid unnecessarily raising the interviewee's level of anxiety. Outlining the purpose of the interview in a brief, straightforward manner reduces the opportunity for the paranoid individual to misinterpret your intent. By substituting the phrase, "I am *working on* the AmeriCon *case*" for something more inflammatory, such as, "I am *investigating* the *bombing* of AmeriCon," you sound less threatening. By conducting the introductory process in this way, you have increased the chances that the paranoid individual will believe that he can expect an open, respectful interview conducted by a competent professional who takes his or her job seriously.

Remember that paranoid individuals believe the world is a hostile and dangerous place in which others are out to take advantage of them in some way. Think of the interview within this context. The interview environment now becomes their "world," and you represent potential harm. As previously discussed, their assumptions are that they cannot trust you, you are out to harm them, and all your actions are nothing more than attempts to attack, trick, or deceive. One strategy they often use to deal with these beliefs is to attack. So, although you may do all you can to lower anxieties, be prepared for your interviewee to go on the offensive with behavior that can be angry, hostile, sarcastic, condescending, or accusatory. This could happen at the outset of the interview or at any point in which he feels threatened in any way. In the face of such behavior, maintain a calm, professional, and neutral stance that keeps the interview on track. The following examples are illustrative:

Paul Jones: I'm not stupid. I watch the news. Do you think I have forgotten Waco or Ruby Ridge? I know how the government works. I know what you're trying to do here.

Mr. Jones' attack and his implication that the interviewer cannot be trusted are immediate and delivered with substantial emotion. It puts you at an important choice-point, one at which awareness and control of your instinctive response of angry defensiveness could make the difference between the interview continuing or shutting down.

An example of a defensive response that might confirm the paranoid individual's assumptions:

Interviewer: Don't believe everything you see in the news. I've been in law enforcement for fifteen years and I've heard all of that before from people who either don't know what they're talking about or who just like to engage in conspiracy theories.

An example of a nondefensive response:

Interviewer: I'm not going to argue with you, Mr. Jones. Since I wasn't involved in either of those incidents, I don't have the kinds of facts I like to work with. But both of those incidents involved loss of life, and that's always a tragic outcome. Now, I'd like to ask you about...

In the above example, the nondefensive response calmly addresses the interviewee's beliefs without refuting or discounting them, but without substantially reinforcing them either. That is very different from a defensive response that tries to put the law enforcement agent in a one-up position by questioning and demeaning the interviewee's perceptions.

Because paranoid individuals see themselves as potential victims in a threatening and dangerous world, they typically feel that their aggressive behavior, even if it breaks the law, is fully justified. Therefore, you need to find a way to legitimize these thoughts and feelings in the mind of the interviewee without agreeing with him. One way to do this is by "reflecting" these feelings back. In essence, this involves repeating the *theme* of his statement in a way that appeals to his sense of victimization while neither dismissing nor agreeing with it. Consider the following example:

Interviewer: It sounds like you felt your company was not being understanding.
Paul Jones: Of course they weren't. They were going to garnish my wages. They wouldn't listen to anything I said. They took the side of the judge and my ex-wife.
Interviewer: It seems you made every effort to resolve this.
Paul Jones: I wrote letters. I made phone calls. I went to every government office I could think of. I even contacted an attorney. No one would help me. I think they are all in it together. All they want is to take my money and ruin me.
Interviewer: As you saw it, you'd done everything you could think of and nobody would listen or help you.

The examples above demonstrate several important points. First, the strategic use of reflection allows the interviewee to maintain his sense of victimization. Second, by not contradicting or dismissing the interviewee's feelings, you keep him focused on substantive issues rather than on you. Third, the use of reflection gives you the opportunity to be empathic in a very subtle way. Obvious attempts at empathy, such as physically moving closer or using phrases such as "I know how you feel" or "I understand how you feel," can often elicit swift, negative reactions. However, by using language such as "It sounds like…," "It seems…," and "As you saw it…," you convey understanding in a nonemotional way. While gaining the paranoid interviewee's trust is next to impossible, the examples above reflect an impartial stance that might be enough to create the environment you need for a successful interview.

Hand in hand with the sense of being victimized is the tendency of paranoid individuals to place the blame for their behavior on others, including the victims of their aggression. We previously discussed the importance of being prepared not to respond with outrage if this occurs. For example, Mr. Jones might insinuate that the administrative assistant who was injured opening the pipe bomb package was not an innocent victim. This is because, in his mind, everyone who worked at that company was part of a network whose aim was to harm him. Once again, you are at a choice-point. Instead of acting on the instinctive anger that such an insinuation would naturally elicit, calmly reflecting the person's perceptions while neither refuting nor agreeing with them will serve to keep the interview on track. For example,

Interviewer: You saw her as part of the overall problem with the organization.

—or—

Interviewer: Your sense was that she was the same as everybody else. Could you tell me more about exactly what happened?

We want to make an important point here. Due to the nonjudgmental manner in which you conduct an interview with a paranoid individual, he may come away feeling that the interviewer has agreed with his beliefs and condoned his behavior. Therefore, it is extremely important that, *if he is going to be released at the end of the interview,* you make it very clear that you cannot condone or allow any behavior on his part that would potentially harm anyone. For example,

Interviewer: Mr. Jones, I understand where you were coming from. However, any behavior that could potentially harm somebody is unacceptable and would result in serious consequences for you, and I'm sure that is something neither of us wants.

The above example makes it clear to the interviewee that further aggressive behavior will not be tolerated. However, the language and the tone used by the interviewer convey the message in a nonthreatening way, which leaves the door open for any subsequent interview.

Key Points to Remember

Do

- Do present a verbal outline of what will be covered during the interview (e.g., "We'll start by getting some biographical information and then I want to ask you about the events of August 16th.").
- Do script out succinct, straightforward questions beforehand.
- Do be open and direct.
- Do be professional.
- Do be patient and tolerant.
- Do be brief (i.e., complex statements leave room for misinterpretation).
- Do be confident without being arrogant and condescending.
- Do be tolerant of the interviewee's need for boundaries.

Don't

- Don't take accusations personally.
- Don't react emotionally.
- Don't try to defend yourself against the interviewee's hostility.
- Don't do all the talking.
- Don't be ambiguous.

- Don't be excessively friendly or supportive.
- Avoid saying, "I know how you feel."
- Avoid directly challenging perceptions or beliefs.

References

American Psychiatric Association. (2000). *Diagnostic and statistical manual of mental disorders (4th ed., text rev.)*. Washington, DC: American Psychiatric Association.

Auchincloss, E.L., and Weiss, R.W. (1992). Paranoid character and the intolerance of indifference. *Journal of the American Psychoanalytic Association, 40*, 1013–1037.

Shapiro, D. (1965). *Neurotic styles*. New York: Basic Books.

Shea, S.C. (1998). *Psychiatric interviewing: The art of understanding (2nd ed.)*. Philadelphia: W.B. Saunders.

THE SCHIZOTYPAL PERSONALITY

Peter Walker had been working as a nighttime janitor at the local high school for the past several years. His mother worked in the cafeteria. She had helped Peter get the job after he had been quite unsuccessful in finding one on his own. During his job interview, it was difficult for him to stay on track with even the basic information about himself. He rambled on about having a sixth sense and being able to read people's minds. Even more surprising was his appearance. Peter showed up for the interview looking disheveled, wearing clothes that looked like he had picked them out of his laundry hamper. Despite the minimal supervision during the night shift and the fact that he appeared to be a bit of an odd duck, the principal thought he was harmless enough. Also, given that the principal knew his mother, he felt a bit more confident about offering Peter the job.

Peter had given college a try, but it just was not for him. He struggled not only with the coursework, but also with having to sit in the classroom with the other students. While he always wanted to be a part of the group, it seemed that every time he opened his mouth or approached someone, it backfired. This was especially the case when he started talking about his telepathic abilities or his ability to predict the future.

Working at the high school was a good fit for him, as he did not feel anxious because he was rarely around others. He was also able to listen to his favorite radio station and his favorite DJ, Marie Summers (a.k.a. Midnight Marie). He had been listening to her show for some time, and he knew that every time she played the national anthem at midnight, it was for him. One night, he was listening to her and after she played the national anthem, she began laughing. She had never done that before. He knew she was laughing at him. It brought back all the bad feelings he had when other people laughed at him, and he began having negative thoughts about her. The following week she announced on her show that her father had just died. Peter immediately knew that he had caused her father's death because of his negative thoughts. He decided to write to her and let her know what happened. He had written her several times but never received any response, and he was starting to feel frustrated. Peter figured that maybe the post office was not delivering his mail to her or that someone was throwing his letters away.

He could not believe it when he saw a flyer announcing that Marie Summers was coming to the school to give a lecture to the broadcasting club. He knew he would have to approach her and let her know that he had been writing to her. Peter showed up early for work that afternoon so he would not miss her. He sat in the very back of the library, hidden behind some books, and listened to her lecture. He learned about her childhood and education. He could not believe it when she said she was born in California, just the same as him.

After the lecture, several students approached her to ask questions. He waited for the room to empty out and slowly approached her while she was packing up her things. Rather than introducing himself, he launched right into a discussion about how he had unusual powers and abilities, and was able to read people's minds. He also said that for a long time he had been able to communicate with the dead. As soon as she heard this, she immediately recognized the odd and unusual manner of his speech and connected it to the bizarre letters she had received over the past several months. She remembered one particular letter that had bothered her a great deal, because it talked about being able to communicate with her dead father. While there was no specific threat in the letter, it made her feel uncomfortable and concerned that this individual might be stalking her.

Peter was rambling on about his special and magical powers when somehow he mustered up the nerve to ask her out to dinner.

She panicked and ran off. He followed her, grabbed her by the arm, and continued explaining his unique abilities. As usual, he failed to recognize the awkwardness of the situation. To make matters worse, he also made comments about how it was his fault that her father died. Marie became frightened by Peter's persistence and his comments about her father's death. She went directly to the principal's office, and he (the principal) immediately called the police.

The police responded to the school and spoke with Marie Summers, who told them what had happened. Given the incident and background information, one of the detectives decided to interview Peter Walker.

Describing the Schizotypal Personality

The current *Diagnostic and Statistical Manual of Mental Disorders* (DSM-IV-TR) includes nine items in its description of Schizotypal Personality Disorder; however, they all revolve around four main concepts: acute social discomfort, a reduced capacity for close relationships, cognitive or perceptual distortions, and eccentricities of behavior. Frances et al. (1995) noted that schizotypal individuals are typically withdrawn and demonstrate eccentric beliefs, paranoid tendencies, idiosyncratic speech, perceptual illusions, unusual appearance, inappropriate affect, and social anxiety (p. 368). Schizotypal individuals come across as peculiar, eccentric, and bizarre. Because of their awkwardness, social situations rarely go well, and their level of anxiety in those situations is substantial. They are often loners, not by choice, but because of the frequent rejection they encounter when they try to make contact. They are often left with feelings of emptiness and disconnectedness.

Schizotypal personality falls on the schizophrenic continuum. While these individuals share characteristics with schizophrenics such as disorganized thinking, they differ from schizophrenics in that they do not experience the hallmark symptoms of frank hallucinations and bizarre delusions that would likely lead to a diagnosis of schizophrenia, and they generally function at a somewhat higher level. However, the disorganized thinking and poor logic that characterizes the schizotypal personality can lead to very inaccurate conclusions and behavior. For example, when Peter Walker assumed that Marie Summers played the national anthem for him and that she was laughing at him when she laughed after playing it, he linked unrelated events into a network of unique meaning for himself (ideas of reference).

Schizotypal individuals also struggle with interpersonal relationships. They are generally not capable of interpreting and communicating the range of emotion necessary for successful interaction. These individuals have a difficult time reading cues and understanding social norms, resulting in inappropriate behavior—such as Peter Walker's attempt to restrain Marie Summers as she tried to leave. They may appear internally preoccupied or distracted and have trouble expressing their thoughts and emotions coherently. When they try to engage in conversation, they may ramble from topic to topic or go off on tangents that are difficult for others to follow. This decreased ability to interact appropriately can be off-putting, resulting in few friendships or intimate relationships.

Many believe the most striking feature of individuals with schizotypal personality disorder is their odd thought processes. Beck (1990) describes four types of abnormal cognition, including suspicious or paranoid ideation, ideas of reference, odd beliefs and magical thinking, and illusions.

These individuals sometimes attempt to validate their odd beliefs by suggesting that they have telepathic abilities or a psychic aptitude that allows them to communicate with the dead or predict the future. They also report being superstitious and overly involved in paranormal activity. They sometimes claim that they have magical abilities that can influence others, like Peter Walker's conviction that his negative feelings about Marie Summers caused her father's death. Schizotypal individuals may state that they are able to feel when someone is present and that they sense that things are going to happen before they actually do.

Schizotypal individuals also have significant issues regarding their physical presentation that may be off-putting to others. Their unusual mannerisms and poor hygiene compromise their ability to find work or form relationships, resulting in further isolation and ostracism.

In summary, schizotypals exhibit the following features:

- Odd, unusual, and bizarre thoughts and beliefs
- The belief that they have unique abilities such as telepathy or magical control over others' thoughts
- Ideas of reference
- Severe social discomfort and anxiety that does not improve as they feel more comfortable in their surroundings
- Suspiciousness and paranoid ideation
- Odd perceptual experiences that fall short of bizarre hallucinations and delusions
- Unusual and eccentric mannerisms and appearance
- A lack of close friendships or intimate relationships

Assessing the Schizotypal Personality

This section is not designed to exhaust all sources of information you may utilize to conduct an indirect assessment of a potential interviewee. Rather, it is designed to suggest a number of questions that address the core features of the schizotypal personality and offer some recommendations about sources of information typically useful in answering those questions. Remember that these questions are *not* for the purpose of diagnosing the interviewee with Schizotypal Personality Disorder, but rather for determining the presence and strength of schizotypal features of his or her personality. For convenience, this section is written for the assessment of a male interviewee, but the suggestions are equally relevant for women.

One of the central features of the schizotypal personality is a sense of social discomfort and awkwardness. When interviewing family and friends, be sure to ask about his behavior within social settings. The following questions may be useful to explore:

- Does he tend to avoid social situations because they make him anxious?
- Would you describe him as distant or aloof?
- Does he sometimes believe that people are thinking or talking about him (even when they are not)?
- Does he seem to get nervous when he has to engage in small talk?

- Does he prefer to be by himself?
- Is he quiet in social settings?
- Does he rarely laugh or smile?
- Is his nonverbal communication poor (e.g., unusual manner-isms, lack of eye contact)?
- Does he seem to be nervous in a group of people?
- Does he have unusual manners or behaviors? Do these become worse when he is under stress or feeling anxious?
- Are his expressions inconsistent with the situation? (For example, in a situation where it would be typical to feel sad-ness or grief, does he appear unaffected or nonchalant?)

Schizotypal individuals tend not to develop close relationships with others due to their unusual thoughts and behaviors. This does not mean that they do not desire contact with others, but rather that they simply are not able to obtain it because of their unusual cognition and peculiar behavior. Over time, the difficult experi-ences they have had with others lead to a sense of distrust and suspiciousness. When interviewing others, try to find out what the schizotypal individual's attitudes and behaviors are regarding relationships:

- Does he think that people pretend to be his friend in order to take advantage of him?
- Does he have a hard time figuring out what people really mean?
- Do people tell him that he reads too much into things?
- Do people tell him that he takes offense at things that were not meant to be critical?
- Does he have any close friends that he can confide in (exclud-ing his immediate family)?
- Does he make people around him feel anxious or uncomfortable?
- Does he have little interest in getting to know other people?
- Does he say that others have a hard time understanding what he means when he is talking?
- Does he seem to be on guard even with those he is closest to?
- Does he believe that friends and coworkers are really not trustworthy?

- Does he often find other people's comments to be threatening or demeaning?

The schizotypal person also has unusual cognitive processes, including bizarre speech and magical thinking. These individuals also may believe they have a sixth sense or are able to read other people's minds. So, when talking with others, consider the following questions:

- Does he believe that television programs or newspaper articles have special meaning for him?
- Does he often talk about having supernatural experiences?
- Does he believe that he is telepathic (able to read other people's minds)?
- Does he talk about having some type of entity (e.g., person or force) around him even though others cannot see it?
- Is he concerned that others may be able to read his mind or tell what he is thinking?
- Does he believe in clairvoyance (e.g., psychic issues, fortune telling)?
- Does he state that objects, events, or people seem to have a special meaning just for him?
- Is he superstitious?
- Does he ramble when he talks?
- Does he wander off topic when speaking?
- Is his speech vague and often difficult to follow?
- Does he feel that other people's conversations have special meaning for him (e.g., ideas of reference)?

Preparation Issues

Preparation is a critical aspect of any interview. The intent of this section is to provide you with an understanding of those issues that are important considerations as you prepare to interview the schizotypal personality.

Understanding Your Reactions to the Individual

Before conducting the interview, it is important to understand the instinctive ways in which you are likely to respond to the schizotypal personality. These are individuals who are uncomfortable and awkward in social situations. Not only do they exhibit tangential and magical thinking, but they may often have an unusual appearance accompanied by peculiar mannerisms. These individuals have been ostracized from mainstream society because of their oddness, so they are used to others responding to them in a negative manner. You too are likely to feel confused by or critical of their behavior. However, if you respond in a perplexed or judgmental manner, you serve to further reinforce their prior experiences and justify their negative reactions within the interview setting.

Anxiety for these individuals can have an incapacitating effect on their overall ability to function, especially with regard to logical thinking and interpersonal relationships. When placed under significant stress (e.g., being involved with law enforcement), their thoughts and behavior may further fragment and become even more odd, eccentric, and tangential. Millon et al. (2004) noted that "as anxiety increases, they may retreat further behind a curtain of disordered communication as a means of shielding themselves and confusing the intruder" (p. 431).

In interviewing schizotypal individuals, it is important to be aware of your own potential to become angry, frustrated, or confused by their inability to communicate clearly and to answer your questions directly. Although it may be difficult, it is critical that you allow them to express their thoughts without getting lost in the disjointed nature of them. Due to their tendency to ramble, it is not uncommon for interviewers to become impatient with what might surely become a challenging and lengthy interview. In addition, there may be extended periods of silence, which can sometimes make interviewers uncomfortable. Remember to exercise patience and not be offended by silence. Impatience will only validate their expectations of a hostile interviewer or authority figure. They may need the periods of silence as a respite to help maintain their composure, reduce their anxiety, and organize their thoughts.

Because of their difficulty relating, you may also feel disconnected from the schizotypal interviewee. As a result, you may become bored or frustrated and begin to withdraw. At times, you may also feel like you are interviewing someone who is almost childlike and become frustrated with the person's inability to meet your adult expectations.

However, if you start to feel this way, try to modify your expectations regarding the capabilities of schizotypal individuals and go back to basics. Recall their limitations and be patient. If you see that the person is becoming overwhelmed, offer to take a break or have a family member sit in on the interview to help alleviate anxiety. You may also want to review your questions to ensure that you are asking clear and concise questions that are not complex or compounded.

These individuals also have an incredibly difficult time structuring their environment under normal circumstances, let alone an anxiety-producing setting such as a forensic interview. As the interviewer, you need to establish the parameters of the interview and help guide them along. When they become lost in their thoughts, you must gently redirect them back to the question at hand. Most important, you need extreme patience when approaching an interview with a schizotypal individual.

Who Should Conduct the Interview

Understanding the schizotypal personality and what you are likely to encounter within the interview setting is critical in conducting an effective interview. It is equally critical that you possess the right combination of personality traits or features given the information discussed up to this point in order to have the best chance at a successful outcome.

First and foremost, the interviewer must possess tremendous patience, focus, and critical thinking skills. Given the level of baseline anxiety that schizotypal individuals possess, in addition to their tendency to ramble on about unrelated topics, a lengthy interview can be expected. Not only will it take time for the interviewer to calm (as much as possible) the individual's level of anxiety, but it may also take time to sort through the information to glean any useful details. The interviewer must avoid getting sidetracked by the interviewee's rambling and loose associations and be able to continually separate what is factual from what is a product of his or her distorted thought processes.

The interviewer should also be someone who can convey a sense of openness and tolerance, especially when the schizotypal individual makes unusual references and engages in magical or superstitious thinking. This is necessary because schizotypal individuals often perceive others as intrusive, judgmental, attacking, or humiliating (Millon et al., 2000). Along with patience and tolerance, the interviewer should be capable of maintaining a calm demeanor and not letting feelings or emotions show. Despite the schizotypal individual's bizarre claims, odd mannerisms, elaborate speech, and eccentric appearance, it is crucial that the interviewer tolerate potential feelings of frustration, confusion, irritation, amusement, disbelief, skepticism, or any other feelings that may arise without expressing them outwardly.

The interviewer should also be someone who is able to communicate in clear and straightforward language. Schizotypal individuals have difficulty organizing their thoughts. Therefore, the interviewer needs to structure the interview and help the person stay on track. By using unambiguous, concise, and organized language, the interviewer may be able to minimize opportunities for misperceptions. Try not to leave anything open to interpretation, even while recognizing that the schizotypal individual may still take things the wrong way or misinterpret your responses.

Gender and age can be critical to a successful interview. A schizotypal individual may feel more comfortable with someone who is older, as opposed to a peer. He is more likely to be closely connected with his immediate family such as his mother or father. Therefore, a motherly or fatherly figure may be most desirable. Keep in mind, however, that if you possess the qualities described above, gender and age become less of a factor.

As always, a thoughtful, honest self-evaluation on the part of the interviewer is crucial. Typically, the law enforcement officer assigned to the case is likely to conduct the interview. If, however, it is determined that someone else would be better suited to conduct the interview, that determination should take precedence in order to increase the likelihood of the interview's success.

Number of Interviewers

It is recommended that you have only one interviewer because of the schizotypal person's extreme social discomfort and anxiety. The fewer the number of interviewers, the easier it is for the interviewee to attempt to manage his anxiety. If, however, there are two interviewers, one should be designated the primary interviewer while the second one should be solely responsible for taking notes. The second interviewer's role should be discussed with the interviewee so that he does not become suspicious of his or her intentions. We would strongly discourage involving more than two interviewers.

Physical Space/Environment/Interpersonal Space

If you have the luxury of conducting the interview away from a law enforcement facility, you should choose one that does not appear to the interviewee to give you an advantage. For example, in the vignette above, the police chose to interview Peter Walker at the school to minimize his anxiety. If they had transported him to the police station, he likely would have become so anxious and overwhelmed that he would have had a difficult time producing useful information. If possible, make sure to keep the environment free of distractions (e.g., people, outside noise, office clutter), given the fact that schizotypals are vulnerable to being overwhelmed by excessive stimulation.

It is also important to respect the interviewee's personal space. These are individuals who have become suspicious and distrusting. They sometimes worry that others can intrude on their minds as well as their bodies. Therefore, you do not want to invade their personal space during the interview. You can set up the room in a number of ways, to include a table between you or appropriate space if you are only using chairs. A number of these options will work. However, whichever one you choose, make sure you are able to maintain a buffer zone. While this may seem subtle to you as the interviewer, it will make a significant difference in the schizotypal individual's overall comfort level.

Nonverbal Behavior

The important thing to remember is that you do not want your nonverbal behavior to give away what you are feeling regarding any particular issue. As mentioned in previous chapters, think of the interview as a poker game. This is a time where you need to maintain a calm exterior and the ultimate "poker face." Do not let your behavior give away any negative emotions (e.g., judging, disapproving, disbelief) or any positive emotions (e.g., overfriendliness) that you may experience during the course of the interview. In addition, your nonverbal behaviors should convey the message that you are attentive and respectful without being overly friendly or intrusive. Also, you do not want your nonverbal behaviors to be interpreted as attacking, dismissive, or disapproving. For example, if he begins talking about his telepathic abilities, be sure that you are not shaking your head, sighing heavily, or rolling your eyes. Always be aware of your own behaviors and what they are communicating to the interviewee.

Questions

Because schizotypal individuals have an extremely difficult time understanding and navigating interpersonal relationships, it is important to keep questions basic, unambiguous, and straightforward. Even with standard demographic questions, these individuals may struggle to provide coherent responses or have trouble connecting the purpose of the interview with the questions being asked. Therefore, make sure you have a structured line of questioning prepared for the interview. This can ensure that you are clear, concise, and unambiguous while also helping you to stay on track with your questioning. In this way, you keep your place and will be better prepared when the interviewee takes you on a verbal detour. Furthermore, by having something prepared that is clear and straightforward, it minimizes the chance for misinterpretation on the part of the interviewee.

Recording the Interview (Notetaking, Audio/Video Recording)

While notetaking is important in many interviews, it is less important when interviewing schizotypal individuals. Because of their cognitive difficulties, it may be more important to focus on the individual and gently guide him through the interview while maintaining a structured and comfortable environment. Information will likely not be provided at such a rate that you will need to refer back to your notes. However, you may find notetaking useful when the person begins rambling about an unrelated topic, as it may help you recall the question at hand. Notetaking then becomes a tool to help the interviewer record what is factual while allowing the schizotypal interviewee to integrate his feelings and perceptions without getting lost in circuitous and disjointed thinking. This interview may feel like you are "pulling teeth" to get the information you need. Therefore, more focus should be placed on keeping the individual engaged in the interview than on copious notetaking.

Audio and video recording are recommended. This should be addressed as a matter of policy in order to ensure the accuracy of the interview for the protection of the interviewee. Regardless of whether you use audio or video recording, notetaking is still recommended for the aforementioned reasons.

Time Frame

As previously mentioned, it is important to set aside a significant period of time when interviewing a schizotypal individual. The person will likely never become comfortable in the setting, so the goal is to minimize anxiety as much as possible. There are many factors that impact the time frame. These include whether or not the interviewee is in a custodial situation, the facts of the case known at the time, the nature and extent of the evidence, and the cooperative nature of the interviewee, just to name a few. When your case is highly circumstantial (lacking physical evidence) or there are a number of details in which you feel the interviewee would be vague or inconsistent (or omit altogether), then you may want to consider conducting several low-key, nonthreatening interviews. The interview should not be too fast-paced and should be low key. Approaching the schizotypal person too fast or applying too much pressure can result in severe cognitive, interpersonal, and behavioral disturbances. These individuals are not likely to respond well to high-pressure techniques. Instead, they may further fragment and become more tangential and disorganized in their thoughts. This will only serve to make a lengthy interview even longer.

The Interview

Now that you have a good understanding of the behaviors that schizotypal individuals are likely to engage in during the interview process and the reasons for those behaviors, settled on an effective interview style, and engaged in thorough preparation, it is time for the actual interview. This section cannot be a comprehensive discussion of everything you may encounter, but it will address many of the details that increase the likelihood of the interview going well. In this section we use the vignette of Peter Walker to emphasize key points made throughout the chapter.

As discussed, schizotypal individuals are not comfortable within social situations, particularly with unfamiliar individuals. They become increasingly anxious when authority figures are present, so being interviewed by police will only make what is already a stressful situation even worse. Therefore, it is critical that you are mindful of this as you approach the interview and do everything possible to manage their anxieties. Remember that the notion of minimizing an individual's anxiety level during an interview may seem counterintuitive to law enforcement. However, it will likely be an effective strategy when dealing with schizotypal personality features that can easily become overwhelmed when they are stressed.

These are individuals who have only connected with a few people in the world and those connections are often poor. Frequently, they feel most comfortable with family members, so if it is within the realm of possibility, you may want to consider having a family member sit in on the interview. Including a family member (if appropriate to the situation) may help reduce the individual's level of anxiety and increase the chances of the interview going well. For example, referring to the vignette of Peter Walker, you may want to consider having his mother present during the interview. Recall that she works at the school and was instrumental in getting him the position. Just her presence in the room may help alleviate his extreme social discomfort and improve his ability to function within the interview setting. By incorporating familiarity, you can create a more comfortable environment for the interviewee, enabling him to remain calm and think more coherently. Similarly, arranging the interview in a location that is familiar to the interviewee can also be helpful. In the case of Peter, holding the interview at the school where he is employed, or perhaps at his mother's house, are options that could create a comfortable environment.

Another way in which you can reduce the interviewee's level of anxiety is to minimize your position of power as much as possible. This can be accomplished in several ways. One way is by conducting the interview at a neutral location as described above. Another way is through physical appearance, by making sure that your badge and weapon are not exposed or by not wearing a uniform or any other insignia that affiliates you with power and authority. A third way you can minimize your position of power is by the language you use. For example, when entering the room, you might acknowledge him by stating his name, but shaking his hand might be too intrusive. Consider the following example in the case of Peter Walker:

Interviewer: Peter? Is it okay if I call you Peter?
Peter: Yes.
Interviewer: My name is Dan Martin and I am with the Police Department. I wanted to talk to you about your interactions with Marie Summers. We've asked your mom to sit in with us while we talk with you. Is that okay with you?

Addressing the schizotypal individual by his first name may be helpful in trying to create a more comfortable setting without being overly intrusive or disrespectful. Approaching him in this manner may help set the initial tone of the interview as one of warmth and concern. You immediately showed Peter you are concerned about his needs by telling him that you have asked his mother to sit in on the interview and then asking if he approves. You also identified yourself and told him the purpose of the interview in a clear and concise manner. However, by leaving off your professional rank or title (e.g., Detective, Officer), you accomplish your objective in a nonthreatening way. Words like "talk" and "interaction" are neutral words that do not necessarily suggest that he is potentially in trouble. By using this more casual, nonthreatening language, you decrease the formality and perhaps lower his anxiety in the process.

Ease into the interview and avoid language that emphasizes the seriousness of the situation or that is overly negative (e.g., critical, punitive). As mentioned previously, schizotypal individuals are highly anxious and sensitive to rejection, so avoiding this can help to keep things going in a more positive direction. A good way to ease into the interview is to try to obtain some basic demographic background. This will be useful in a variety of ways. Initially, it will help to determine how well he is able to respond to standard, non-threatening questions. Second, it will also help familiarize him with the interview environment and help get him talking. Consider the following example:

Interviewer: Peter, I need to ask you some basic information about your background. Can you tell me where you're currently living?

Peter: I live over on West Street. I've lived there my whole life. I've never lived anywhere else, so I know everything about the house. The house feels cold at night and so I turn the temperature up higher, but that old radiator doesn't get very warm anymore. Dad says to leave it alone but I can't because it's always cold in my room and I don't have enough blankets. My warmest blanket is the blue one but sometimes I take it to the basement when I watch television down there and forget to bring it—

Interviewer (interrupt and redirect to the question at hand): Okay Peter, can you tell me who lives in your house with you?

Peter: My mom and dad.

Interviewer: Good. Have you ever lived alone?

In this exchange, we see that Peter has a difficult time directly answering the interviewer's questions. While it may be tempting to ask more about his lifestyle, do not undermine the interview structure, as this may be a slippery slope that may open the door for more tangential thoughts. As previously discussed in the chapter, it is difficult for schizotypal individuals to organize and structure their thoughts, so it is particularly important for you to establish the parameters of the interview by having scripted questions that keep the interview on track. In the case of Peter Walker, after speaking with the principal and Ms. Summers, it may be worthwhile for the investigators or officers to take a few minutes and identify the critical information they need to obtain in order to establish some questions to address during the interview. Then, when you see that the individual is digressing or losing focus, you can gently bring them back to the question at hand.

If the schizotypal individual alludes to his supernatural or telepathic abilities during the course of the interview, it is recommended that you be tolerant of this peculiar cognitive process. Rather than directly refuting his magical abilities, the interviewer should simply redirect the individual to the question at hand. You should try to resist the urge to contradict his telepathic or extrasensory abilities and, instead, use it as an opportunity to acquire additional information. Schizotypal individuals may believe that their negative behaviors could have a severe impact on the interviewer. However, if these are verbalized, it will provide you with an opportunity to address his concerns and then tactfully refute them. For example,

Peter: I can read your mind, and I know what you're thinking; and you think I caused her father's death. I have that kind of power, you know.

Interviewer: Of course you're interested in what I'm thinking, just as I'm interested in what you're thinking. I'm interested in how you knew Ms. Summers was coming to your school.

The interviewer responds in a manner that is courteous and empathetic. He acknowledges what Peter says but does not get into a discussion of whether or not he actually possesses those abilities. Instead, the interviewer provides an empathetic yet neutral, factual statement. He simply says, "You're interested in what I'm thinking." This is neither positive nor negative and clearly is not judgmental. Also keep in mind that engaging in a discourse about his extrasensory abilities may divert the interview and may unnecessarily extend what will most likely be a lengthy interview.

As the interview continues, you need to obtain more detailed information about his recent behaviors. It is recommended that you explore these behaviors in a nonconfrontational, nonthreatening, and nonjudgmental manner. Consider the ongoing interview with Peter Walker:

Interviewer: Can you tell me when you first contacted Ms. Summers?

Peter: A couple of months ago. It's bad. I know that it's bad. I was thinking that today; and look, something bad has happened. I always can tell when something bad is going to happen. I hope nothing bad happens to her.

Interviewer: That's why we're here talking; we don't want anything bad to happen to Ms. Summers or to you. Can you tell me how long ago you first wrote Ms. Summers a letter?

Peter: Am I in trouble?

Interviewer: Peter, I'm going to do everything I can to help, but I need to know some more information. When did you first write to Ms. Summers?

Peter: Last March, I think.

Interviewer: Good, Peter.

In this example, you are trying to get more substantive information from Peter. However, he begins to lose focus and exhibits some magical thinking, believing that his thoughts had caused something bad to happen. The interviewer does not reinforce these thoughts or even explore them. He simply states that we do not want anything bad to happen to anyone, including Peter. Peter also asks the interviewer if he is in trouble. The interviewer wisely does not address this directly, but instead provides him with reassurance that he will do everything he can to help. And again, notice that the interviewer structures the interview and redirects back to the question at hand. Also notice that the second time the interviewer asks this question, he becomes a bit more specific. We see that Peter is then able to answer the question. By not responding to or becoming critical of irrelevant information or tangential thoughts, you are maintaining the open and accepting environment that increases the likelihood of a successful interview.

The above exchange also highlights the need for an appropriate pace. It is clear that it is going to take some time to obtain all the necessary information, but pushing too hard could result in decompensation or withdrawal. An interview technique exerting too much pressure too quickly could result in the following:

Interviewer: Can you tell me when you first contacted Ms. Summers?

Peter: It's bad; I know that it's bad. I was thinking that today; and look, something bad has happened. I always can tell when something bad is going to happen. I hope nothing bad happens to her.

Interviewer: Are you saying that something bad is going to happen to her? Are you threatening her?

Peter: She knows I love when she plays the national anthem at night; she was playing it for me. I knew it the first time I heard it, and I knew she knew I was thinking of her the whole time.

Interviewer: How could she possibly know that? You've never even met her before today? Look, I don't have time to play games. When did you first contact her?

Peter: (Silence, then humming).

Interviewer: Peter, you'd better answer my questions, or we're going down to the police station and you can answer me there.

Here we see the interviewer's frustration leaking through, pushing Peter too hard to obtain information that he may not recall. We see that when the interviewer begins exerting a great deal of pressure, Peter retreats into his internal world and completely withdraws from the interview. Again, the interviewer responds in a frustrated manner and begins threatening. This pattern of escalation will likely not result in increased cooperation from Peter. Instead, it will likely increase anxiety and impact the interviewee's ability to provide the information. In this scenario, he is not being deceptive or evasive. He is just not able to organize his thoughts and present them in a manner that is useful and begins to decompensate as the pressure increases.

As a reminder, during the course of the interview with someone with schizotypal features, it is important to remain patient, be tolerant, and not allow your feelings of frustration to come through when you are faced with their tangential responses or nonsensical answers.

In addition, keeping in mind that while it may seem counterintuitive to try to reduce anxiety during the interview, it is critical with these individuals in order to ensure that they do not become overwhelmed and unable to function.

Key Points to Remember

Do

- Do be extremely patient.
- Do be flexible and tolerant.
- Do be empathetic and understanding.
- Do structure the interview to help the person stay on track.

Don't

- Don't take it personally.
- Don't use high-pressure strategies.
- Don't invade their personal space.
- Don't be overly friendly.
- Don't try to increase their already high level of anxiety.
- Don't be dismissive.

References

American Psychiatric Association. (2000). *Diagnostic and statistical manual of mental disorders (4th ed., text rev.)*. Washington, DC: American Psychiatric Association.

Beck, A., Freeman, A., and Davis, D. (2007). *Cognitive therapy of personality disorders (2nd ed.)*. New York, NY: Guilford Publications, Inc.

Frances, A.J., First, M.B., and Pincus, H.A. (1995). *DSM-IV guidebook*. Washington, DC: American Psychiatric Press.

Millon, T., Grossman, S., Millon, C., Meagher, S., and Ramnath, R. (2000). *Personality disorders in modern life (2nd ed.)*. Hoboken, NJ: John Wiley & Sons, Inc.

Raine, A. (1991). The Schizotypal Personality Questionnaire (SPQ): A measure of schizotypal personality based on DSM-III-R criteria. *Schizophrenia Bulletin, 17*, 555–564.

Appendix A

The Dimensional View of Personality

As stated in Chapter 1, the purpose of this book is to provide a window into the personalities most commonly encountered in forensic and law enforcement settings, and to demonstrate how this insight can help in planning and conducting effective interviews. In each chapter we discussed a specific type of personality, the traits and features that form the core of that personality, and implications for effective interviewing. In this appendix we want to provide a more detailed understanding of the dimensional approach to personality description.

Personality: A Constellation of Traits

Personality, in general, is best defined as a constellation of traits. All of us share the same basic traits; however, those traits play out differently, both qualitatively and quantitatively, for each of us. In other words, the nature (quality) and strength (quantity) of any given trait varies from one person to the next. One person might be highly conscientious (quality) and make that an important part of daily function (high quantity). Another person might be equally conscientious (quality) but not spend much time thinking about issues associated with conscientious function (lower quantity). Figure A.1 and Figure A.2 illustrate this concept and provide a visual depiction of personality as a sort of a Venn diagram of overlapping circles. The overall personality depends on not only the nature and strength of each individual trait, but also on how each of these traits interacts with other traits.

In each of these figures, the large center circle represents the overall personality and the smaller circles represent individual traits. The strength of each trait is indicated by how much it overlaps the center circle. For example, the personality in Figure A.1 has a high level of emotional control while the personality in Figure A.2 has a low level of emotional control. The traits of empathy, emotional control, susceptibility to emotional distress, entitlement, anxiety, impulse control, and trust are represented in both personalities. However, the strength

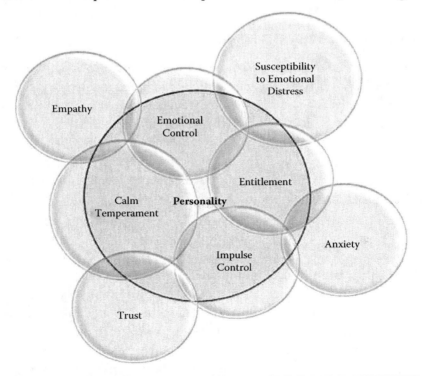

Figure A.1   Personality A as a constellation of traits.

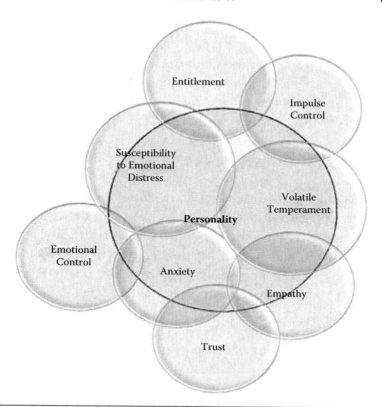

Figure A.2 Personality B as a constellation of traits.

of those traits differs in each, as does the nature of the trait. How the strength and relationships of the individual traits might affect the overall personalities is described below.

Personality A (Figure A.1) possesses high levels of entitlement, emotional and impulse control, and temperamental calmness, and low levels of empathy, anxiety, trust, and susceptibility to emotional distress. An individual with this personality might function fairly well in social and employment settings (high levels of impulse and emotional control), may feel he deserves special recognition and treatment (high level of entitlement), and may use others for his own benefit (high level of entitlement and low level of empathy). Add in the additional low levels of trust, anxiety, and susceptibility to emotional distress, and you have a picture of an individual who would most likely fall at the oblivious end of the narcissistic continuum described in Chapter 2 (and maybe moving along the continuum from oblivious narcissist to disciplined psychopath described in Chapter 4).

Personality B (depicted in Figure A.2), on the other hand, possesses low levels of emotional and impulse control and trust, high levels of susceptibility to emotional distress and anxiety, and has a fairly volatile temperament. An individual with this personality would probably not function as well in social and employment settings (high level of anxiety and low levels of emotional and impulse control). The medium level of empathy indicates an ability to attach emotionally to others; however, low levels of trust, impulse control, and emotional control, high levels of anxiety and susceptibility to emotional distress, and a volatile temperament suggest that intimate relationships would probably be characterized by emotionally intense and unstable behavior. This is a picture of someone with features of the borderline personality described in Chapter 5.

The traits described above represent only a fraction of the total number of traits an individual may possess. As you can imagine, there is an infinite number of possibilities as to what type of personality might emerge as well as the strength of that personality.

The Personality Continuum: Style versus Disorder

The examples provided in the previous section illustrated how the difference in the nature, strength, and interrelationships of the same traits between individuals can result in different personalities. They can also determine where any given personality falls on a continuum from mild to extreme, which is depicted in Figure A.3.

For the purposes of illustration, let's look at the paranoid personality in relation to this continuum. On the left end of the continuum are those individuals who, for the most part, possess mild traits of the paranoid personality and exhibit a paranoid *style*. The more severe, pervasive, and disruptive the traits, the further along the continuum the individual may fall. At the right end of the continuum are those

Figure A.3 The personality continuum.

individuals who possess extreme levels of these traits and exhibit a paranoid personality *disorder.*

For example, the core trait (or feature) of the paranoid personality is a low level of trust. As such, individuals with a paranoid style would exhibit mild levels of distrust, while individuals who are at the disordered end of the continuum would exhibit extreme levels of distrust. The individual with paranoid personality style may be wary of others' motives but could develop close relationships with one or two individuals that he feels have earned his trust. The paranoid personality disordered individual does not develop close relationships because he believes people cannot be trusted. The individual with paranoid style may have higher than normal expectations of loyalty and honesty, but will require substantive evidence before making any accusations. The paranoid disordered individual will accuse others based merely on suspicions not supported by any factual material. The individual with paranoid style will place a premium on fidelity but can achieve some level of trust, whereas the paranoid disordered individual will engage in controlling behaviors based on a strongly held belief that friends or intimate partners will be unfaithful (Millon et al., 2004).

An individual can fall anywhere along this continuum, and determining where personality style ends and personality disorder begins is not an easy distinction to make. Generally speaking, the distinction is made when the behavior starts to become maladaptive, which means it begins to cause problems in work, social, or interpersonal settings. For each of the personalities in this book, the examples we gave fell toward the extreme end of the continuum because as traits become more extreme, they become more maladaptive, and the subsequent behavior becomes more problematic. The more problematic the behavior, the more likely it is that the individual will have some involvement with forensic or law enforcement settings.

The Relationships Between Personality Types

Borderline, Narcissistic, and Antisocial Personalities

There are ten personality disorders described in the *Diagnostic and Statistical Manual of Mental Disorders* ([DSM-IV-TR]; American

Psychiatric Association, 2000). These ten personality disorders are further divided into three groups or "clusters": Cluster A, Cluster B, and Cluster C. The personality disorders within each cluster share certain traits with one or more of the other disorders in that same cluster. Each disorder also has certain traits that distinguish it from the other disorders.

Of the personalities described within this book, borderline, narcissistic, antisocial, and psychopathic personalities are the four that are most often associated with criminal offenders, particularly those who engage in violent offenses. Borderline, narcissistic, and antisocial personalities are part of the Cluster B disorders in the DSM-IV-TR. They share a number of similar features but also differ in significant ways. The best way to conceptualize the relationships and distinctions between borderline, narcissistic, and antisocial personalities is to look at Figure A.4.

The horizontal continuum represents stability of self-esteem (as well as self-image), while the vertical continuum represents the ability to function well in employment, social, and interpersonal settings; and the ability to control emotions, level of impulse control, and level of self-discipline.

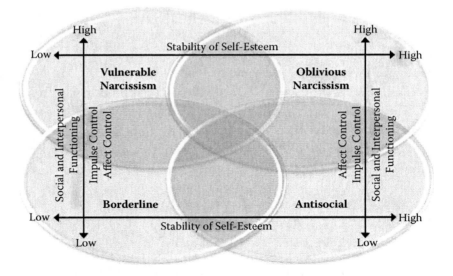

Figure A.4   The borderline, narcissistic, and antisocial continuum.

On the left end of the continuum are borderline and vulnerably narcissistic personalities. They share self-esteem and self-image problems; however, vulnerable narcissists typically possess a greater ability than borderline individuals to control their impulses and emotions. In addition, vulnerable narcissists show a better overall level of general functioning than borderline individuals, who tend to experience severe problems in employment, social, and interpersonal settings.

On the right end of the continuum are obliviously narcissistic and antisocial personalities. They both exhibit relative stability regarding their self-esteem and self-image. However, oblivious narcissists possess a greater ability than antisocial individuals to control their impulses and emotions, and they tend to show more stability and better functioning in employment, social, and interpersonal settings.

At the top of the continuum are the narcissistic personalities. Both the vulnerable and oblivious narcissists function fairly well in employment, social, and interpersonal settings. However, the vulnerable narcissist shows a high level of instability in self-esteem while the oblivious narcissist maintains a relatively stable and high level of self-esteem.

At the bottom of the continuum are the borderline and antisocial personalities. They both exhibit low levels of impulse and emotional control, as well as problems functioning in employment, social, and interpersonal settings. However, the borderline personality exhibits severe self-esteem and self-image problems while the antisocial personality maintains a relatively stable and adequate level of self-esteem.

Figure A.4 does not represent all the traits that these personality types share, or all of those that distinguish one from the other. Rather, several primary traits were chosen to illustrate these similarities and distinctions in order to emphasize the dimensional approach to describing personality. It is also intended to visually demonstrate that an individual can fall anywhere within this continuum (horizontally, vertically, or diagonally). A more in-depth assessment of each of these personalities (and individual traits) is provided in Chapter 2 ("The Narcissistic Personality"), Chapter 3 ("The Antisocial Personality"), and Chapter 5 ("The Borderline Personality").

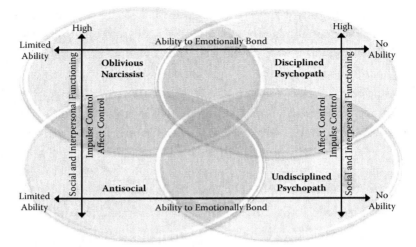

Figure A.5   The narcissistic, antisocial, and psychopathic continuum.

Narcissistic, Antisocial, and Psychopathic Personalities

While psychopathy is not listed as a personality disorder in the current edition of the DSM-IV-TR (although it is likely that it will be included in the next edition of the DSM), it is closely associated with antisocial and narcissistic personalities. Figure A.5 illustrates the relationships between narcissistic, antisocial, and psychopathic personalities.

The horizontal continuum represents the ability to bond emotionally with others, including those emotions (e.g., love, sadness, empathy, sympathy, compassion, guilt, and remorse) and qualities (e.g., loyalty, commitment, and responsibility to and for others) associated with genuine attachment. The vertical continuum represents the ability to function well in employment, social, and interpersonal settings; and the ability to control emotions, level of impulse control, and level of self-discipline.

On the left end of the continuum are the obliviously narcissistic and antisocial personalities. As previously stated, they both exhibit relative stability regarding their self-esteem and self-image. However, they differ in their abilities to control their impulses and emotions, as well as their ability to function in employment, social, and interpersonal settings.

On the right end of the continuum are the psychopathic personalities. Both types share an inability to emotionally bond to others. As such, they do not feel empathic emotions (e.g., love, sadness, empathy, sympathy, compassion, guilt, and remorse) or possess empathic qualities (e.g., loyalty, commitment, and responsibility to and for others) that develop primarily through genuine emotional attachment to others. However, they differ in that disciplined psychopaths have a greater ability than undisciplined psychopaths to control their impulses and emotions and to function adequately in employment, social, and interpersonal settings.

At the top of the continuum are the obliviously narcissistic personality and the disciplined psychopath. Both have the ability to function fairly well in employment, social, and interpersonal settings. However, the oblivious narcissist has some ability (although limited) to bond emotionally with others while the disciplined psychopath is incapable of such attachment.

At the bottom of the continuum are the antisocial personality and the undisciplined psychopath. Both tend to have difficulties functioning well in employment, social, and interpersonal settings. The distinction between the two is that the antisocial personality, like the oblivious narcissist, has some ability (although limited) to bond with others while the undisciplined psychopath has virtually no ability for attachment.

Figure A.5 does not represent all the traits that these personality types share, or all of those that distinguish one from another. Rather, several primary traits were chosen to illustrate these similarities and distinctions in order to emphasize the dimensional approach to describing psychopathy in relation to obliviously narcissistic and antisocial personalities. It is also intended to visually demonstrate that an individual can fall anywhere within this continuum (horizontally, vertically, or diagonally). A more in-depth assessment of this continuum and the relationships between psychopathy, oblivious narcissism, and antisocial personality is provided in Chapter 4 ("The Psychopathic Personality").

The Borderline, Narcissistic, Antisocial, Psychopathic Continuum

Figure A.6 represents an overall picture of the relationships described above between narcissistic, antisocial, borderline, and psychopathic personalities.

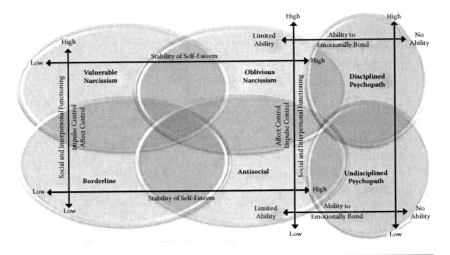

Figure A.6.   The narcissistic, antisocial, borderline, and psychopathic continuum.

The information in this appendix does not address all the personalities discussed within this book. It is intended only to provide a basic understanding of how to conceptualize personality from a dimensional perspective.

References

American Psychiatric Association. (2000). *Diagnostic and statistical manual of mental disorders (4th ed., text rev.).* Washington, DC: American Psychiatric Association.

Millon, T., Millon, C.M., Meagher, S., Grossman, S., and Ramnath, R. (2004). *Personality disorders in modern life.* Hoboken, NJ: Wiley.

Appendix B: Glossary

Affect: Emotional response—positive, negative, or neutral—associated with some experience.

Affective violence: Aggression associated with an intense emotional experience.

Anxiety: The subjective experience of apprehensiveness or panic in the absence of an external stimulus.

Assessment: The systematic evaluation of an individual. *Indirect assessment* involves evaluation through interviews with collateral sources and review of available records without direct access to the individual.

Attachment: Formation of an emotional bond with another.

Delusions: Unrealistic beliefs in the absence of supporting evidence.

Empathy: The ability to understand another person's experience.

Fear: Emotion associated with the awareness of obvious danger.

Grandiosity: Unrealistically positive self-opinion and strongly held view of one's superiority.

Hypervigilance: Excessive monitoring of the behavior of others.

Idea of reference: Belief that objects, events, or the behavior of others have specific meaning for the individual.

Illogical thinking: Thinking containing internal contradictions resulting in erroneous conclusions, sometimes associated with a delusional belief.

Illusion: The perceptual distortion of an actual object or experience.

Magical thinking: Belief that a person's thoughts could cause or prevent some specific event.

Personality: Longstanding pattern of traits and behaviors associated with how an individual views self, others, and the environment.

Personality disorder: Inflexible and pervasive behavior patterns that create significant impairment in the individual's social, interpersonal, and vocational function.

Predatory violence: Violence associated with a calculated opportunity for personal gain or reward; sometimes called *instrumental violence.*

Rapport: Establishment of a positive interpersonal relationship.

Self-concept: The comprehensive image one has of oneself.

Sympathy: Identification with the difficulties and problems experienced by another.

Index